Getting Started with Microsoft® Visual C++™ 6 with an Introduction to MFC

Companion to *C++ How to Program, 2/e*

Deitel & Deitel
Books and Cyber Classrooms
published by
Prentice Hall

How to Program Series
Java™ How to Program, 3/E
C How to Program, 2/E
C++ How to Program, 2/E
Visual Basic® 6 How to Program
Internet and World Wide Web How to Program

Multimedia Cyber Classroom Series
Java™ Multimedia Cyber Classroom, 3/E
C & C++ Multimedia Cyber Classroom, 2/E
Visual Basic® 6 Multimedia Cyber Classroom
Internet and World Wide Web Multimedia Cyber Classroom

The Complete Training Course Series
The Complete Java Training Course, 3/E
The Complete C++ Training Course, 2/E
The Complete Visual Basic 6 Training Course
The Complete Internet and World Wide Web Programming Training Course

Visual Studio® Series
Getting Started with Microsoft® Visual C++™ 6 with an Introduction to MFC
Visual Basic® 6 How to Program
Getting Started with Microsoft® Visual J++® 1.1

To communicate with the authors, send email to:

`deitel@deitel.com`

For information on corporate on-site seminars and public seminars offered by Deitel & Associates, Inc. worldwide, or to purchase a copy of any Deitel publication, visit:

`http://www.deitel.com`

For continuing updates on Prentice Hall and Deitel & Associates, Inc. publications, visit the Prentice Hall web site

`http://www.prenhall.com/deitel`

For volume purchases of Deitel/Prentice Hall publications, please see instructions in the last pages of this book for contacting Prentice Hall directly.

Getting Started with Microsoft® Visual C++™ 6 with an Introduction to MFC

A Companion to *C++ How to Program, 2/E*

H. M. Deitel
Deitel & Associates, Inc.

P. J. Deitel
Deitel & Associates, Inc.

T. R. Nieto
Deitel & Associates, Inc.

E. T. Strassberger
Strassberger Software
Training, Inc.

PRENTICE HALL, Upper Saddle River, New Jersey 07458

Acquisitions Editor: *Petra J. Recter*
Production Editor: *Camille Trentacoste*
Managing Editor: *Eileen Clark*
Executive Managing Editor: *Vince O'Brien*
Chapter Opener and Cover Designer: *Tamara Newnam Cavallo*
Buyer: *Pat Brown*
Editorial Assistant: *Sarah Burrows*

© 2000 by Prentice-Hall, Inc.
A Pearson Education Company
Upper Saddle River, New Jersey 07458

Printed in the United States of America

10 9 8 7 6 5 4 3

ISBN 0-13-016147-0

Prentice-Hall International (UK) Limited, London
Prentice-Hall of Australia Pty. Limited, Sydney
Prentice-Hall Canada Inc., Toronto
Prentice-Hall Hispanoamericana, S.A., Mexico
Prentice-Hall of India Private Limited, New Delhi
Prentice-Hall of Japan, Inc., Tokyo
Prentice-Hall of Asia Pte. Ltd., Singapore
Editora Prentice-Hall do Brasil, Ltda., Rio de Janeiro

To Susanne Peterson

Manager of University Curriculum Programs
Microsoft Research Unit
Microsoft Corporation

and our mentor at Microsoft. Thank you for your extraordinary efforts in the conception and implementation of our

Visual Studio Series

of academic textbooks including

Visual Basic 6 How to Program
Getting Started with Microsoft Visual C++ 6
    with an Introduction to MFC

and our forthcoming titles

Visual J++ 6 How to Program
Visual C++ 6 How to Program
Visual InterDev™ 6 How to Program.

Your enthusiasm, expertise, market savvy and commitment to this series has made creating these books a sheer joy.

Thank you for being the special person that you are.

Harvey, Paul and Tem

To the Smith family

To whom I owe a debt of gratitude that can never be repaid.
Tem

To my wife Linda

For everything and forever.
Ed

Contents

Illustrations

Preface

Welcome to Visual C++ and the exciting world of *Microsoft Foundation Classes (MFC)!* This book is by four guys—HMD (Massachusetts Institute of Technology 1967), PJD (MIT 1991), TRN (MIT 1992) and ETS (University of Maryland 1969) who have been programming and/or teaching for 38, 16, 16 and 36 years, respectively. We got together to produce a book we hope you will find a valuable supplement to our book, *C++ How to Program: Second Edition* (ISBN # 0-13-528910-6), and to its optional multimedia companion, *The Complete C++ Training Course: Second Edition* (ISBN #0-13-916305-0).

Getting Started with Visual C++ 6 with an Introduction to MFC does not teach C++ programming. Rather it assumes that you know C++ or are learning it from any ANSI/ISO C++ textbook such as *C++ How to Program: Second Edition.*

This textbook is part of a package we designed in cooperation with Microsoft to help you start creating, editing, and evolving C++ applications in the Microsoft Visual C++ 6 integrated development environment (IDE). The source code for all the MFC program examples in this book can be downloaded from our website

```
http://www.deitel.com
```

Click the *Downloads* link to access the source code for all our books.

The vast majority of programs in *C++ How to Program: Second Edition* successfully compile with the Microsoft Visual C++ 6.0 compiler. A listing of the few programs that do not compile properly, as well as appropriate fixes can be found on our web site at

```
http://www.deitel.com/products_and_services/
publications/
```

Click the link on this page for *Getting Started with Visual C++ 6 with an Introduction to MFC.*

For technical support with any of our CD-ROMs or interactive *Multimedia Cyber Classrooms*, please contact Prentice Hall at

```
tech_support@prenhall.com
```

They respond promptly during regular business hours (East Coast Time; United States).
We will be happy to answer your programming language questions via email at

```
deitel@deitel.com
```

We hope you enjoy this book and programming in Microsoft's Visual C++ 6 integrated development environment with MFC!

Why We Wrote *Getting Started with Visual C++ 6.0 with an Introduction to MFC*

C++ How To Program: *Second Edition* teaches ANSI/ISO C++ programming—an internationally used language that does not provide capabilities for creating graphical user interfaces (GUIs). Many of our readers have asked us to prepare a supplement that would introduce the fundamental concepts of *Microsoft Windows programming* (i.e., creating graphical user interfaces and writing graphics-intensive programs) using MFC. Our adopters asked us to use the same "live-code" approach (i.e., teaching each concept in the context of complete working example programs followed by the screen dialogs) that we employ in all our *How to Program Series* textbooks. Our goal was clear: produce a Visual C++ 6 book for introductory university-level C++ programming courses that would supplement *C++ How to Program: Second Edition* or any other ANSI/ISO C++ textbook, and would introduce fundamental MFC GUI-and-graphics programming concepts.

Our Approach to Presenting MFC

The *Microsoft Foundation Classes (MFC) library* is a large collection of classes that help Visual C++ 6 programmers quickly create powerful Windows-based applications.

MFC programming is a substantial and complex topic. Various 1000-page MFC books are available for full-semester advanced programming courses. Our book is not intended as an alternative to these. Rather it is intended as a supplement to the introductory/intermediate-level programming courses typically taught from generic ANSI/ISO C++ textbooks like our *C++ How to Program: Second Edition*. Most colleges do not teach MFC programming in these courses. But several have told us that they would like to offer a brief introduction to Windows programming with MFC in their C++ courses. Chapter One of the book describes how to create and run MFC-based programs using Microsoft's Integrated Development Environment (IDE).

Visual C++ provides so-called *wizards* to generate a program's *skeletal code* or "*boiler plate*" *code*—the common code that a Windows program requires. The wizards generate this code and then mark the sections where programmers should fill in the code specific to their applications. Experienced programmers like wizards because they enable *rapid application development*. Editing the code generated by a wizard is not a task for beginning MFC programmers. This code is complex and requires a deep understanding of MFC.

We do not use wizards in this book. Our approach is to build the student's understanding of MFC fundamentals gradually by explaining small, narrowly-focused, complete examples. We feel that the student should first see and code small MFC programs to gain a solid understanding of MFC fundamentals. After studying this book, the student can then begin experimenting with wizards.

Teaching Approach

Getting Started with Visual C++ 6 with an Introduction to MFC contains a rich collection of examples, exercises and projects drawn from many fields to provide the student with a chance to solve interesting real-world problems. The book concentrates on the principles of good software engineering and stresses program clarity. We avoid arcane terminology and syntax specifications in favor of teaching by example. Each of our code examples has been carefully tested. This book is written by four educators who spend most of their time teaching edge-of-the-practice topics in industry classrooms worldwide. The text emphasizes pedagogy.

Introducing Object Orientation from Chapter Two!
Getting Started with Visual C++ 6 with an Introduction to MFC "jumps right in" with object-oriented programming and even basic graphical user interface design from Chapter 2! MFC students really want to "cut to the chase." There is great stuff to be done in MFC so let's get right to it! MFC is not trivial by any means, but it's fun and students can see immediate results. Students can get graphical programs running quickly through MFC's extensive class libraries of "reusable components."

Live-Code Teaching Approach
The book is loaded with live-code examples. This is the focus of the way we teach and write about programming, and the focus of each of our multimedia *Cyber Classrooms*. Virtually every new concept is presented in the context of a complete, working MFC program immediately followed by one or more windows showing the program's output. We call this style of teaching and writing our *live-code approach. We use the language to teach the language.* Reading these programs is much like entering and running them on a computer.

World Wide Web Access
All of the code for *Getting Started with Visual C++ 6 with an Introduction to MFC* is on the Internet at the Prentice Hall Web site **http://www.prenhall.com/deitel** and at the Deitel & Associates, Inc. Web site **http://www.deitel.com**. Please download all the code then run each program as you read the text. Make changes to the code examples and see what happens. See how the Visual C++ 6 compiler "complains" when you make various kinds of errors. See the effects of making changes to the code. It's a great way to learn MFC programming by doing MFC programming. [Please respect the fact that this is copyrighted material. Feel free to use it as you study MFC, but you may not republish any portion of it without explicit permission from the authors and Prentice Hall.]

Objectives

Each chapter begins with a statement of *Objectives*. This tells the student what to expect and gives the student an opportunity, after reading the chapter, to determine if he or she has met these objectives. It is a confidence builder and a source of positive reinforcement.

Quotations

The learning objectives are followed by quotations. Some are humorous, some are philosophical and some offer interesting insights. Our students enjoy relating the quotations to the chapter material. The quotations are worth a "second look" after you read each chapter.

Outline

The chapter *Outline* helps the student approach the material in top-down fashion. This, too, helps students anticipate what is to come and set a comfortable and effective learning pace.

Approximately 1,708 lines of code in 17 Example Programs (with Program Outputs)

We present MFC features in the context of complete, working Visual C++ 6/MFC programs. This is the focus of our teaching and our writing. Each program is followed by a window with the output produced when the program runs. This enables the student to confirm that the programs run as expected. Reading the book carefully is much like entering and running these programs on a computer. The programs range from a few lines of code to substantial examples with many lines of code. Students should download all the code for the book from our Web sites (and run each program while studying that program in the text.

53 Illustrations/Figures

An abundance of charts, line drawings and program outputs is included.

40 Programming Tips

We have included programming tips to help students focus on important aspects of program development. We highlight dozens of these tips in the form of *Good Programming Practices, Common Programming Errors, Testing and Debugging Tips, Look-and-Feel Observations, Portability Tips*, and *Software Engineering Observations*. These tips and practices represent the best we have been able to glean from a combined ten decades of programming and teaching experience. One of our students—a mathematics major—told us recently that she feels this approach is like the highlighting of axioms, theorems and corollaries in mathematics books; it provides a basis on which to build good software.

6 Good Programming Practices

When we teach introductory courses, we state that the "buzzword" of each course is "clarity," and we highlight as *Good Programming Practices* techniques for writing programs that are clearer, more understandable, more debuggable, and more maintainable.

7 Common Programming Errors

Students learning a language tend to make certain errors frequently. Focusing the students' attention on these *Common Programming Errors* helps students avoid making the same errors. It also helps reduce the long lines outside instructors' offices during office hours!

11 Testing and Debugging Tips

These tips will help you determine if your program is running correctly and, if not, quickly locate and remove any bugs.

4 Look-and-Feel Observations

We provide *Look-and-Feel Observations* to highlight Windows graphical user interface conventions. These observations help students design their applications to "look" and "feel" like typical Windows programs.

1 Portability Tip

We include a *Portability Tip* to help students write code that will port easily among a variety of MFC-based platforms.

11 Software Engineering Observations

The object-oriented programming paradigm requires a complete rethinking about the way we build software systems. MFC is effective for performing good software engineering. The *Software Engineering Observations* highlight architectural and design issues that affect the construction of software systems, especially large-scale systems. Much of what the student learns here will be useful in upper-level courses and in industry as the student begins to work with large, complex real-world systems.

Summary

Each chapter ends with additional pedagogical devices. We present a thorough, bullet-list-style *Summary* of the chapter. On average, there are 29 summary bullets per chapter. This helps the students review and reinforce key concepts.

Terminology

We include in a *Terminology* section an alphabetized list of the important terms defined in the chapter—again, further reinforcement. On average, there are 85 terms per chapter.

Summary of Tips, Practices, and Errors

For ease of reference, we collect and reiterate the *Good Programming Practices*, *Common Programming Errors*, *Testing and Debugging Tips*, *Look-and-Feel Observations*, *Portability Tips* and *Software Engineering Observations*.

55 Self-Review Exercises and Answers (Count Includes Separate Parts)

Extensive self-review exercises and answers are included for self-study. This gives the student a chance to build confidence with the material and prepare for the regular exercises. Students should be encouraged to do all the self-review exercises and check their answers.

49 Exercises (Count Includes Separate Parts)

Each chapter concludes with a substantial set of exercises including simple recall of important terminology and concepts; writing individual MFC statements; writing small portions of functions and classes; writing complete MFC functions, classes and applications; and writing major term projects. The variety of exercises enables instructors to tailor their courses to the unique needs of their audiences and to vary course assignments each semester. Instructors can use these exercises to form homework assignments, short quizzes, and major examinations. [**NOTE: Please do not write to us requesting the solutions to the exercises. Distribution of the solutions is strictly limited to college professors teaching from the book. Instructors may obtain the solutions only from their regular Prentice Hall representatives.**]

Approximately 1129 Index Entries (with approximately 1942 Page References)
We have included an extensive *Index* at the back of the book. This helps the student find any term or concept by keyword. The *Index* is useful to people reading the book for the first time and is especially useful to practicing programmers who use the book as a reference. Each of the 437 terms in the *Terminology* sections appears in the *Index* (along with many more index items from each chapter). Students can use the *Index* in conjunction with the *Terminology* sections to be sure they have covered the key material of each chapter.

Bibliography
An extensive bibliography is included to encourage further reading.

A Tour of the Book

This book contains five chapters, an Internet and World Wide Web resource appendix, and a bibliography. Each chapter contains examples that carefully illustrate Visual C++ and MFC concepts. Each chapter concludes with a summary, a terminology list, a list of programming tips, self-review exercises (with answers) and exercises (without answers).

Chapter 1: Visual C++ Integrated Development Environment introduces the basics of the Microsoft Visual Studio 6 integrated development environment (IDE); discusses the online documentation; explains how to create, save and execute a *Windows console application* (i.e., an application that does not use graphical user interface elements such as windows and buttons) and discusses the debugger. Helpful integrated development environment features such as s*yntax color highlighting*—the coloring of keywords, comments and values for emphasis—are discussed. This chapter introduces the concept of a *project*—a group of program files associated with an application that resides in a specific directory. All programs compiled in Visual C++ use projects.

   The debugger helps programmers find code that, although it does not violate C++ syntax, contains *logic errors* (e.g., infinite loops, division-by-zero exceptions, off-by-one errors, etc.) that prevent the program from executing correctly. The debug toolbar and menu contain the tools necessary to debug a C++ application. Capabilities such as watching variable values change as a program executes are discussed. Chapter 1 is designed to be taught as early as possible in your curriculum to allow students to develop programs using the Visual C++ IDE. *Note:* The debugger section references functions and should therefore be taught after Chapter 3 "Functions" in *C++ How to Program: Second Edition.*

Chapter 2: MFC Programming: Part I introduces Windows programming (i.e., creating programs that have GUIs) with MFC and *event-driven programming*—writing code that responds to user interactions with programs (such as button clicks). Each "live-code" example presents one or two new concepts in a short, concise fashion. Each example includes screen captures showing the user's interaction with the program at execution time.

In this chapter we overview some of the classes in the MFC hierarchy. We outline the subset of MFC classes we present in this introductory book. We also provide a "high-level" discussion of MFC events—called *messages*—that describes the code needed for event-driven programming. We introduce the *Hungarian notation* convention for naming identifiers used in Microsoft's MFC documentation and widely practiced in the MFC programming community. We also list (step-by-step) how to create a project for a *Windows application with a graphical user interface* (i.e., a Visual C++ program that uses MFC).

The first program is our classic "Welcome to" program. It introduces the minimal code needed to implement an MFC application. The second example demonstrates how to create menus. The program creates a series of menus containing food-related items. When a food-item is selected, its price is added to a running total. This example introduces message handling and a *message box* window for displaying text to the user. The last "live-code" example introduces the *edit text control* (i.e., a control for accepting input), buttons and dialog-based applications.

Because MFC is a class hierarchy it uses inheritance. Chapters 2 through 5 should be taught after Chapter 9 "Inheritance" in *C++ How to Program: Second Edition.*

Chapter 3: MFC Programming: Part II continues the Windows programming discussion started in Chapter 2. This chapter contains 4 "live-code" examples. The first example demonstrates password protection for edit text controls by masking input with asterisks. In this example, we also enhance message box windows by adding predefined icons. The second example demonstrates how to handle mouse messages. In this example, we demonstrate how to code mouse handlers to determine the coordinates of a mouse click and to determine which mouse button was clicked. This example also introduces basic graphics by drawing directly on the window. The third "live-code" example demonstrates how to code key handlers (i.e., handlers that execute when a key on the keyboard is pressed). In this example, we create a simple text editor. The last example builds upon the graphics techniques introduced earlier in the chapter by drawing centered-red text in the window.

Chapter 4: Graphical User Interface Controls presents 5 MFC controls for enhancing GUIs. We carefully selected these controls based upon our experience with GUI design using Visual J++ and Visual Basic. The set of controls we present is fundamental to Windows programming.

The first "live-code" example demonstrates how to create and use a *multiline edit text* control. This example allows the user to type text into a multiline edit control as if it were a simple text editor. The second example demonstrates toggle controls called *check boxes*. A control—called a *group box*—for grouping other controls is also introduced. The third "live-code" example introduces mutually-exclusive toggle controls called *radio buttons*. This example demonstrates how radio buttons are combined into groups and how they differ from check boxes. The last two examples demonstrate controls (*list boxes* and *combo boxes*) that provide a lists of strings. We discuss how to add strings to these controls and how to remove strings from these controls.

Chapter 5: Graphics. We thought you might enjoy an introductory chapter on graphics, so we went one step further in this book than just introducing GUI programming. Unfortunately, graphics are not included as part of ANSI/ISO C++, so graphics may be a new topic to many C++ programmers. MFC provides a rich collection of classes and functions for creating and manipulating graphics. As with the previous chapters, we have carefully selected introductory MFC features that are demonstrated using five "live-code" examples.

We present the topic of colors that allow graphics to "come-alive" by discussing the *RGB* (red, green and blue) values that form a color. We provide a list of RGB values for common colors in a table.

The first "live-code" example draws a rectangle and a solid-red ellipse in a window. The program demonstrates how to create *brushes* (objects that specify color and fill patterns of an enclosed area) and *pens* (objects that specify line color, thickness and pattern).

The second "live-code" example builds upon the first example by introducing additional brush and pen features and by introducing functions for drawing lines and polygons. This example draws a rectangle and a solid-green arrow in a window.

Our third "live-code" example introduces the *timer object* which sends a message to a message handler after a specified number of milliseconds has elapsed. Timers have numerous applications, especially in graphics where shapes can be drawn at different coordinates when the timer message is received—creating a simple animation. In this example, we animate the colors inside a rectangle by manipulating each individual pixel's color.

The fourth "live-code" example demonstrates how a bitmap image can be displayed in a window and the fifth example introduces fonts. We discuss how to manipulate the font name, size and weight. Font manipulation is important for emphasizing and de-emphasizing text.

Appendix A: Resources and Demos lists some popular sites on the World Wide Web pertaining to Visual C++ and MFC. A *Bibliography* is included to encourage further reading.

Acknowledgments

One of the great pleasures of writing a textbook is acknowledging the efforts of the many people whose names may not appear on the cover, but without whose dedication and hard work producing this textbook would have been impossible.

Our most important source of information was Microsoft's Visual C++ 6 documentation. We owe a special thanks to the skilled technical writers who prepared this material.

We are fortunate to have been able to work on this project with a talented and dedicated team of publishing professionals at Prentice Hall, including Petra Recter (Computer Science Editor) and Sarah Burrows (Editorial Assistant). Camille Trentacoste did a marvelous job as production editor.

We would like to acknowledge the efforts of Barbara Deitel who researched the quotes, prepared the index, located the dozens of valuable Internet and World Wide Web resources in Appendix A, and coordinated the complex reviewer, copy edit and production phases of this book.

We sincerely appreciate the efforts of our reviewers:

Microsoft Reviewers:

Jeff Ressler	Microsoft Corporation
David Schwartz	Microsoft Corporation

Academic Reviewers:

Bob McGlinn	Southern Illinois University Carbondale
Jesse Heines	University of Massachusetts at Lowell
Uday Kulkarni	Arizona State University
Douglas Troy	Miami University
Richard Albright	University of Delaware

Industry Reviewers:

Ajay Kalra	Autodesk, Inc.
Don Kostuch	You Can C Clearly Now
Jonathan R. Earl	Technical Training and Consulting
Barry L. Wallis	Science Applications International Corp.
Richard M. Reese	Traverse Technologies
Chris Scott	SnoopSoft Corporation
Siamak Amirghodsi	Black Dot Group
Bob Powell	Rogue Wave Software Inc.
David J. Wilkinson	Efficient Solutions Inc.

Under an especially tight time schedule, they scrutinized every aspect of the text and made countless suggestions for improving the accuracy and completeness of the presentation.

We owe special thanks to the creativity of Tamara Newnam Cavallo who did the art work for our programming tip icons and the cover. She created the delightful bug creature who shares with you the book's programming tips.

We owe a great to deal Susanne Peterson of Microsoft who sponsored our efforts and moved mountains to help us form this unique product for you.

We would greatly appreciate your comments, criticisms, corrections and suggestions for improving the text.

Please address all comments to our email address:

deitel@deitel.com

Harvey M. Deitel
Paul J. Deitel
Tem R. Nieto
Edward T. Strassberger

Sudbury, Massachusetts
June, 1999

About the Authors

Dr. Harvey M. Deitel, CEO of Deitel & Associates, Inc., has 38 years experience in the computing field including extensive industry and academic experience. He is one of the world's leading computer science instructors and seminar presenters. Dr. Deitel earned

B.S. and M.S. degrees from the Massachusetts Institute of Technology and a Ph.D. from Boston University. He worked on the pioneering virtual memory operating systems projects at IBM and MIT that developed techniques widely implemented today in systems like UNIX, Windows NT and OS/2. He has 20 years of college teaching experience including earning tenure and serving as the Chairman of the Computer Science Department at Boston College before founding Deitel & Associates, Inc. with Paul J. Deitel. He is author or co-author of several dozen books and multimedia packages and is currently writing several more. With translations published in Japanese, Russian, Spanish, Basic Chinese, Advanced Chinese, Korean, French, Polish and Portuguese, Dr. Deitel's texts have earned international recognition. Dr. Deitel has delivered professional seminars internationally to major corporations, government organizations and various branches of the military.

Paul J. Deitel, Executive Vice President of Deitel & Associates, Inc., is a graduate of the Massachusetts Institute of Technology's Sloan School of Management where he studied Information Technology. Through Deitel & Associates, Inc. he has delivered Java, C and C++ courses for industry clients including Compaq, Digital Equipment Corporation, Sun Microsystems, Rogue Wave Software, Hitachi, Stratus, Fidelity, Cambridge Technology Partners, Open Environment Corporation, One Wave, Hyperion Software, Lucent Technologies, Adra Systems, Entergy, CableData Systems, NASA at the Kennedy Space Center, the National Severe Storm Laboratory, National Oceanagraphic and Atmospheric Administration (NOAA), White Sands Missle Range, IBM and many others. He has lectured on C++ and Java for the Boston Chapter of the Association for Computing Machinery. He is the co-author of fifteen books and multimedia packages with Harvey Deitel and is currently writing several more.

The Deitels are co-authors of the world's best-selling introductory college programming language textbooks, *C How to Program: Second Edition*, *C++ How to Program: Second Edition* and *Java How to Program: Third Edition*. The Deitels are also co-authors of the *C & C++ Multimedia Cyber Classroom: Second Edition*—Prentice Hall's first multimedia-based computer science textbook, the *Java Multimedia Cyber Classroom: Third Edition* and the *Visual Basic 6 Multimedia Cyber Classroom* co-authored with their colleague Tem R. Nieto. Their book, *Internet and World Wide Web How to Program* (Prentice Hall; December 1999), presents an intense, college-level treatment of programming principles and multitier software development in the context of the Internet and the World Wide Web. The related publication (for Windows), *The Complete Internet and World Wide Web Programming Training Course*, will be published in January 2000.

Tem R. Nieto, Principal Instructor with Deitel & Associates, Inc., is a graduate of the Massachusetts Institute of Technology where he studied engineering and computing. Through Deitel & Associates, Inc. he has delivered courses for industry clients including Sun Microsystems, Digital Equipment Corporation, Compaq, Stratus, Fidelity, Art Technology, Progress Software, Toys "R" Us, National Oceanographic and Atmospheric Administration, Jet Propulsion Laboratory, Nynex, Motorola, Federal Reserve Bank of Chicago, Banyan, Schlumberger, University of Notre Dame, NASA, Nasdaq, various military installations and many others.

Edward T. Strassberger, President of Strassberger Software Training, Inc. is a graduate of the University of Maryland, College Park, where he studied engineering and information systems. He has 36 years experience in the computer field developing operating systems, compilers, networks, and data modeling and statistical analysis applications.

About Deitel & Associates, Inc.

Deitel & Associates, Inc. is an internationally recognized corporate training, publishing and educational consulting organization specializing in programming languages, object technology, and Internet and World Wide Web software technology education. The company offers courses on Java™, C++, C, Visual Basic®, Smalltalk, Object-Oriented Analysis and Design, MFC, COM, DCOM, ActiveX™, CORBA, and various Internet and World Wide Web software development technologies. The principals of Deitel & Associates, Inc. are Dr. Harvey M. Deitel and Paul J. Deitel. The company's clients include many of the world's largest computer companies, government agencies, branches of the military and business organizations. Through its publishing partnership with Prentice Hall, Deitel & Associates, Inc. publishes leading-edge programming textbooks, professional books, interactive CD-ROM based multimedia *Cyber Classrooms, Complete Training Courses* (each including both a textbook and an interactive multimedia package)*, companion Web sites, Web-based courses* and broadcast satellite courses. Deitel & Associates, Inc. and the authors can be reached via email at

`deitel@deitel.com`

To learn more about Deitel & Associates, Inc. and its worldwide on-site and public seminar course offerings, visit:

`http://www.deitel.com`

To learn more about Deitel & Deitel Prentice Hall publications, visit:

`http://www.prenhall.com/deitel`

Visual Studio 6 Integrated Development Environment

Objectives

- To understand the relationship between C++ and Visual C++.
- To be able to use Visual C++ to create, compile and execute C++ console applications.
- To understand and be able to use the Microsoft's Visual Studio 6 integrated development environment.
- To be able to search Microsoft's on-line documentation effectively.
- To be able to use the debugger to locate program logic errors.

If you build it, he will come.
William P. Kinsella

Here Skugg lies snug
As a bug in a rug.
Benjamin Franklin

Change the environment; do not try to change man.
Richard Buckminster Fuller

I do not object to people looking at their watches when I am speaking. But I strongly object when they start shaking them to make certain they are still going.
Lord Birkett

Outline

1.1 Introduction

Welcome to the Visual C++® 6 integrated development environment (part of the *Microsoft Visual Studio® 6* suite of development tools) and an introduction to programming with *Microsoft Foundation Classes (MFC)*. In this chapter you will learn how to create, compile, execute and debug C++ programs using the powerful C++ development environment from Microsoft—*Visual C++ 6*. When you complete this chapter, you will be able to use Visual C++ to begin building applications. Chapters 2 through 5 provide a brief introduction to MFC and creating graphical user interfaces (GUIs). MFC is a deep and complex topic. This book covers MFC at an introductory level that is suitable for use as a companion text in a first year university C++ programming course sequence.

This book does not teach C++; rather, this book is intended as a companion to our textbook *C++ How To Program*, *Second Edition* or any other ANSI/ISO C++ textbook. *C++ How To Program, Second Edition* does not teach GUI programming simply because ANSI/ISO C++ does not provide any libraries for creating GUIs. Compiler vendors such as Microsoft, Borland and Symantec normally provide their own libraries that support creation of applications with GUIs. Many of our readers have asked us to provide a supplement that would introduce the fundamental concepts of *Microsoft Windows programming* (i.e., creating GUIs) using MFC. Our readers asked us to use the same "live-code" approach with outputs that we employ in all our *How to Program Series* textbooks.

There are two versions of this book—an academic and a professional edition. The academic edition—available only to college students—includes the *Microsoft Visual C++ 6 Introductory Edition* software. This product helps students learn C++ in the context of the Microsoft Visual C++ development environment. The professional edition is not bundled with software (Microsoft allows the *Introductory Edition* to be used only in colleges and universities). [*Note:* If you bought the professional edition of this book you will have to purchase separately the *Standard*, *Professional* or *Enterprise Edition* of Microsoft Visual C++ 6. The *Introductory Edition* software provided by Microsoft is not suitable for the heavy-duty software development requirements of professional programmers.]

Before proceeding with this chapter, you should be familiar with the topics in Chapter 1, "Introduction to Computers and C++ Programming," and Chapter 2, "Control Structures," of *C++ How to Program, Second Edition*. A few of the examples in this chapter make reference to *functions*. For these examples, you should be familiar with the material through Section 3.5 of Chapter 3, "Functions," in *C++ How to Program, Second Edition*. Also, one figure in this chapter uses keyword **struct** which is first covered in Section 6.4 of Chapter 6, "Classes and Data Abstraction," in *C++ How to Program, Second Edition*.

We hope you enjoy learning about the Visual C++ 6 integrated development environment and introductory MFC programming with this textbook.

1.2 Integrated Development Environment Overview: Visual C++

Figure 1.1 shows the initial screen image of the *Microsoft Visual C++* integrated development environment (*IDE*). This environment contains everything you need to create C++ programs—an *editor* (for typing and correcting your C++ programs), a *compiler* (for translating your C++ programs into machine language code), a *debugger* (for finding logic errors in your C++ programs after they are compiled) and much more. The environment contains many buttons, menus and other graphical user interface (GUI) elements you will use while editing, compiling and debugging your C++ applications.

1.3 On-line Visual C++ Documentation

Visual C++ 6.0 uses the *Microsoft Developer Network (MSDN*™*)* documentation, which is accessible by selecting **Contents** from the **Help** menu. Microsoft has combined the documentation for all their development tools into MSDN just as they have combined the development tools (e.g., Visual Basic®, Visual C++, Visual J++®, etc.) into one product suite called *Visual Studio®*. Selecting **Contents** displays the ***MSDN Library Visual Studio 6.0*** dialog (Fig. 1.2). The on-line documentation for a C++ or MFC term is also displayed by clicking the word in an editor window and pressing the *F1 key.*

The Visual C++ documentation is also accessible via the World Wide Web at the *Microsoft Developer Network* Web site

```
http://msdn.microsoft.com/library
```

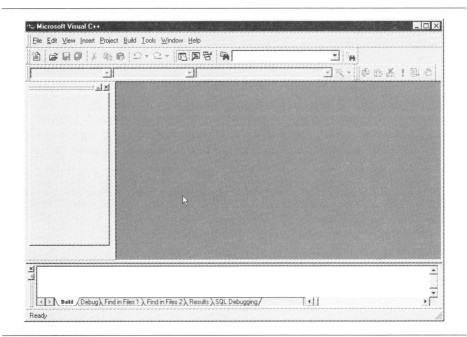

Fig. 1.1   Microsoft Visual C++ IDE.

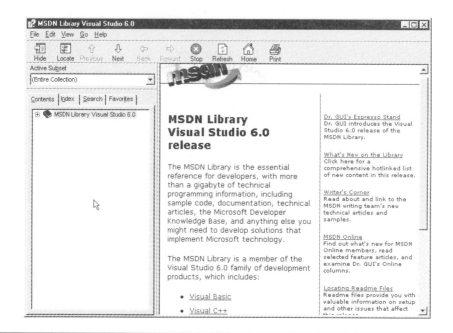

Fig. 1.2 Microsoft Developer Network on-line documentation.

If you have not already registered for the Microsoft Developer Network there, you will be asked to register. There is no charge for registering at the Web site. The documentation is arranged hierarchically. You can find the Visual C++ documentation under

```
Microsoft Developer Network Library
     Visual Studio 6.0 Documentation
          Visual C++ Documentation
```

Information about all aspects of Visual C++ is available. Topics range from the Standard C++ Library to the *Microsoft Foundation Classes* (*MFC*). Topics are displayed in *tree-view format* (see the leftmost portion of Fig.1.3). Clicking the left mouse button on the plus (+) sign next to a topic expands its subtopics. [*Note:* For the rest of this chapter, we refer to *"clicking the left mouse button"* simply as *clicking*.]

The **MSDN Library Visual Studio 6.0** toolbar (the row of icons near the top of the window in Fig. 1.3) is used to navigate through the on-line documentation in a manner similar to viewing pages in a Web browser. In fact, a modified version of Microsoft's **Internet Explorer** Web browser is used to view the documentation. Clicking the left and right arrows on this toolbar move back and forward, respectively, through any previously viewed pages. The **Stop** button causes the program to stop loading the current topic. The **Refresh** button reloads the current topic from the document's source. The toolbar also provides a **Home** button that displays the **MSDN Library Visual Studio 6.0 release** page (Fig. 1.3).

In the left panel, the user can control the display in the right panel by selecting the **Active Subset** of the **MSDN Library** to use and selecting a tab for viewing the **Con-**

tents, *Index*, *Search* or *Favorites*. The *Contents tab* displays the tables of contents. The *Index tab* displays a list of key terms from which to select a topic. The *Search tab* allows a programmer to search the entire on-line documentation contents for a word or phrase. The *Favorites tab* lets the user save links to interesting topics and later return to them.

On-line information is divided into categories. Each category is preceded by a book icon. The *Visual C++ Start Page* is the starting point for navigating the on-line documentation. The *Visual C++ Documentation Map* outlines the various sections of the Visual C++ documentation by category. The *What's New in Visual C++ 6.0* topic explains the newest features introduced in Visual C++ 6.0.

Getting Started with Visual C++ 6.0 contains links to various topics in the documentation, including **Beginning your Program**, **Porting and Upgrading**, **Visual C++ Tutorials**, **What's New for Visual C++ 6.0**, **Getting Help** and **Visual C++ Home Page**. These topics cover a broad range of subjects such that a programmer new to Visual C++, regardless of programming background, can find something of interest.

The *Using Visual C++* category is composed of four subcategories—*Visual C++ Tutorials,* which contains tutorials on how to develop applications that use advanced language features (e.g., OLE server, OLE containers, ActiveX controls, etc.); *Visual C++ Programmers Guide,* which contains information on various programming topics (e.g., portability issues, debugging, errors, etc.); *Visual C++ User's Guide,* which contains information about the Visual C++ IDE (e.g., projects, classes, editors, utilities, etc.); and a *Glossary,* which contains acknowledgments and terminology.

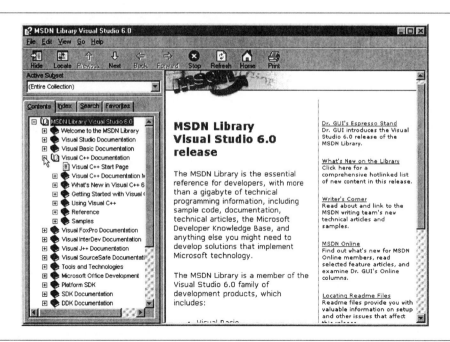

Fig. 1.3   Expanding the Visual C++ topics.

The **Reference** category contains two subcategories—**Microsoft Foundation Class Library and Templates** and **C/C++ Language and C++ Libraries**. The **Microsoft Foundation Class Library and Templates** category contains information about the *Active Template Library (ATL)*—a set of C++ class templates used to develop *distributed applications* (i.e., programs the communicate with each other over a network to perform a task). The category also includes sample programs, technical notes, a hierarchy chart (showing the relationships among the MFC classes) and a class library reference. The **C/C++ Language and C++ Libraries** category contains information about the *Standard Template Library (STL)* [a set of reusable C++ template components that make programming easier], the C++ language, the C language and the standard C++ libraries. The text in a topic is hyperlinked to related text via the Hypertext Markup Language (HTML) technique of highlighting a term with color and underlining it to indicate which words can be clicked to display a definition or other details about a term.

The **Visual C++ Samples** category provides subcategories with example programs for some of the most important features in Visual C++.

1.4 Creating and Executing a C++ Application

You are now ready to begin using the Visual C++ IDE to create a C++ program. In this chapter, we do not create Windows applications that use graphical user interfaces (GUIs) with menus, buttons, etc., GUI programming is introduced in the next chapter. Rather, we create *Win32 console applications*. When executed, Win32 console applications get input from an *MS-DOS window* (a text-only display that predates Windows) and display data to an MS-DOS window. This type of application is used for the example and exercise programs in *C++ How to Program, Second Edition*.

Program files in Visual C++ are grouped into *projects*. A project is a text file that contains the names and locations of all its program files. Project file names end with the **.dsp** (**d**escribe **p**roject) extension. Before writing any C++ code, you should create a project. Clicking the **File** menu's **New...** menu item displays the **New** dialog of Fig. 1.4. The **New** dialog lists the available Visual C++ project types. Note that your **New** dialog may display different project types depending on which Microsoft development tools are installed on your system. When you create a project, you can create a new *workspace* (a folder and control file that act as a container for project files) or combine multiple projects in one workspace. A workspace is represented by a **.dsw** (**d**escribe **w**orkspace) file. The examples in this book have one project per workspace.

Starting with the **New** window, a series of dialog windows guides the user through the process of creating a project and adding files to the project. The IDE creates the folders and control files necessary to represent the project.

From the list of project types, select **Win32 Console Application**. The **Project name** field (in the upper-right corner of the dialog) is where you specify the name of the project. Click in the **Project name** field and type **Welcome** for the project name.

The **Location** field is where you specify the location on disk where you want your project to be saved. If you click in the **Location** field and scroll through it using the right arrow key, you will notice that the project name you typed (**Welcome**) is at the end of the directory path. If you do not modify this directory path, Visual C++ stores your projects in this directory. Although this is not shown, we selected our **D:** drive (we edited the **Location** field to display **D:\Welcome**). You may, of course, choose a different location. You can do this by pressing the browse button (see Fig. 1.4) and navigating to the desired location. Pressing **OK** closes the **New** dialog and displays the **Win32 Console Application - Step 1 of 1** dialog (Fig. 1.5).

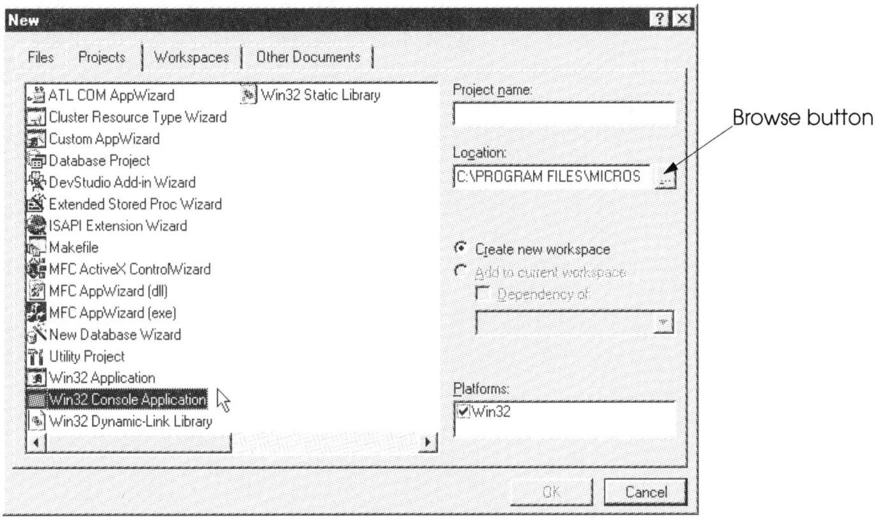

Fig. 1.4   **New** dialog displaying a list of available project types.

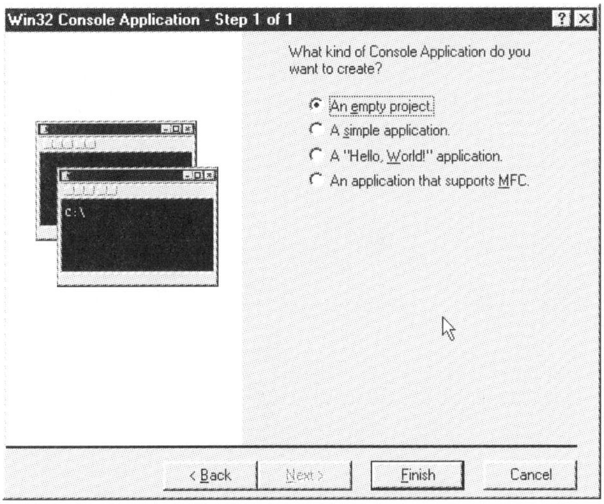

Fig. 1.5   **Win32 Console Application - Step 1 of 1** dialog.

The **Win32 Console Application - Step 1 of 1** dialog displays four choices. Selecting **An empty project** creates a project that does not contain any files. The programmer must add source code files to the project. **A simple application** creates a `.cpp` file (i.e., a file—called a *C++ source file* into which the programmer writes C++ code) and a few support files. Selecting **A "Hello, World" application** creates a `.cpp` file (which contains the code to print **Hello World**) and a few support files. Selecting **An application that supports MFC** creates several files which add support for Visual C++'s Windows programming library called *MFC*. At this point, you should select **An empty project** and click **Finish** to display the ***New Project Information*** dialog (Fig. 1.6). If you selected the wrong project type (i.e., a type other than **Win32 Console Application**) in the **New** dialog and do not see the choices in Fig. 1.5, click **<Back** to view the **New** dialog.

The **New Project Information** dialog provides a summary of the project about to be created. For our **Win32 Console Application**, the dialog specifies that the project is empty (i.e., no additional files were created). This dialog also specifies in the lower-left corner the location on disk for this project. Clicking **OK** closes the dialog and creates the project. If you created the wrong project type, click **Cancel** to go back to the **Win32 Console Application - Step 1 of 1** dialog.

Figure 1.7 shows the Visual C++ IDE after creating an empty **Win32 Console Application**. The IDE displays the project name (i.e., **Welcome**) in the title bar, and shows the *workspace pane* and the *output pane*. If the output pane is not visible, select **Output** from the **View** menu to display the output pane. The output pane displays various information, such as the status of your compilation and compiler error messages when they occur.

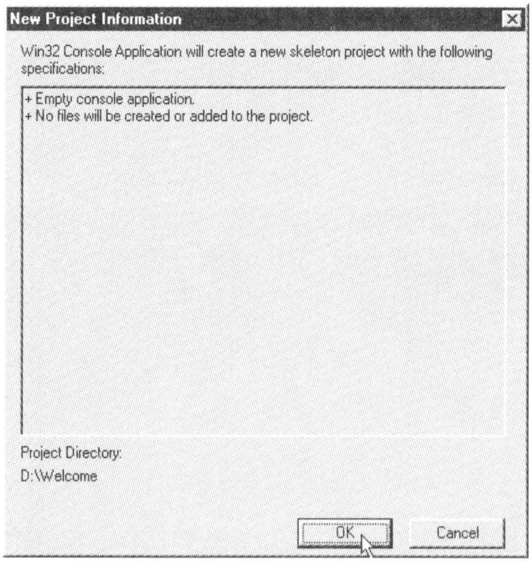

Fig. 1.6   **New Project Information** dialog.

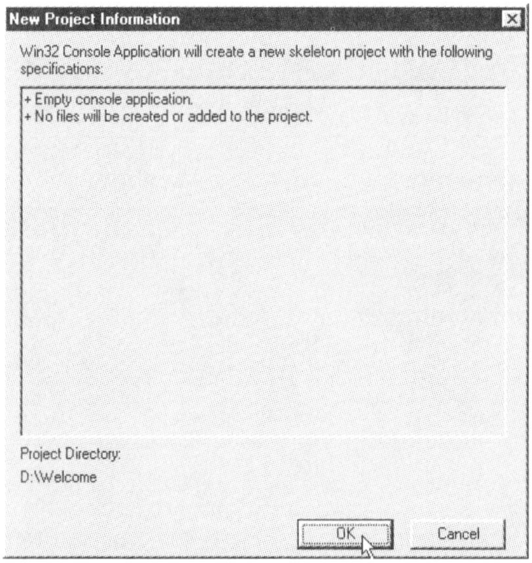

New Project Information   ☒

Win32 Console Application will create a new skeleton project with the following specifications:

+ Empty console application.
+ No files will be created or added to the project.

Project Directory:
D:\Welcome

OK   Cancel

Workspace pane   Title bar

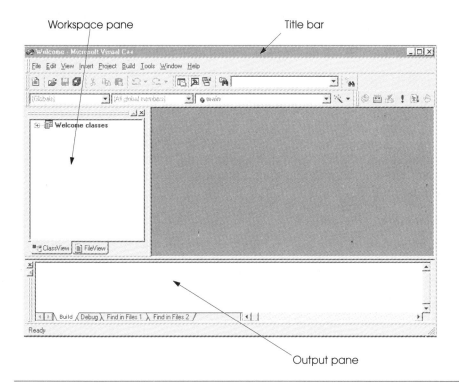

Output pane

Fig. 1.7   Visual C++ IDE displaying an empty project.

At the bottom of the workspace pane are two tabs, *ClassView* and *FileView*. Clicking **ClassView** displays classes and class members (discussed in Chapter 6 of *C++ How To Program: Second Edition*), and functions (discussed in Chapter 3 of *C++ How To Program: Second Edition*) in your project. **FileView** displays the names of the files that make up the project. **FileView** initially displays the project name followed by the word **files** (e.g., **Welcome files**). Clicking the plus sign, **+,** to the left of **Welcome files** displays three empty folders: **Source Files**, **Header Files** and **Resource Files**. **Source Files** displays C++ source files (i.e., **.cpp** files), **Header Files** displays header files (i.e., **.h** files) and **Resource Files** displays resource files (i.e., **.rc** files that define window layouts). For this example we only use the **Source Files** folder.

The next step is to add a C++ file to the project. Selecting **New...** from the **File** menu displays the **New** dialog (Fig. 1.8). When a project is already open, the **New** dialog displays the **Files** tab containing a list of file types. The file types will vary based on the Microsoft development tools installed on your system.

Select *C++ Source File* for a C++ file. The *File name* field is where you specify the name of the C++ file. Enter **welcome** in the **File name** field. You do not have to enter the file name suffix "**.cpp**" because it is implied when you select the file type. Do not modify the **Location** text box. When checked, **Add to Project** adds the file to the project. If **Add to Project** is not checked, check it. Click **OK** to close the dialog. The C++ file is now saved to disk and added to the project. In our example, the file **welcome.cpp** is saved to the location **D:\Welcome** (the combination of the **Location** field and the project name). Figure 1.9, shows the IDE after adding **welcome.cpp** to the project. In Fig. 1.9 we clicked the **+** character next to **Source Files** to see that the C++ source file is indeed part of the project. The plus **+** becomes a minus **-,** and vice versa, when clicked.

Common Programming Error 1.1

Forgetting to add a C++ source file that is part of a program to the project for that program prevents the program from compiling correctly.

We are now ready to write a C++ program. Type the following sample program into the source code window. [*Note:* The code examples for this book are available at the Deitel & Associates, Inc. Web site (**www.Deitel.com**). Click the "downloads" link to go to our downloads page.]

```
#include <iostream.h>

int main()
{
    cout << "Welcome to Visual C++!" << endl;
    return 0;
}
```

The source code window is maximized (also called *docked*) in Fig. 1.9. Click the **Restore** button (see Fig. 1.9) to restore the source code window to its default size.

Testing and Debugging Tip 1.1

*Click in front of a brace (i.e., [or {) or a parenthesis (i.e., () and press **Ctrl +]** to find the matching brace or parenthesis.*

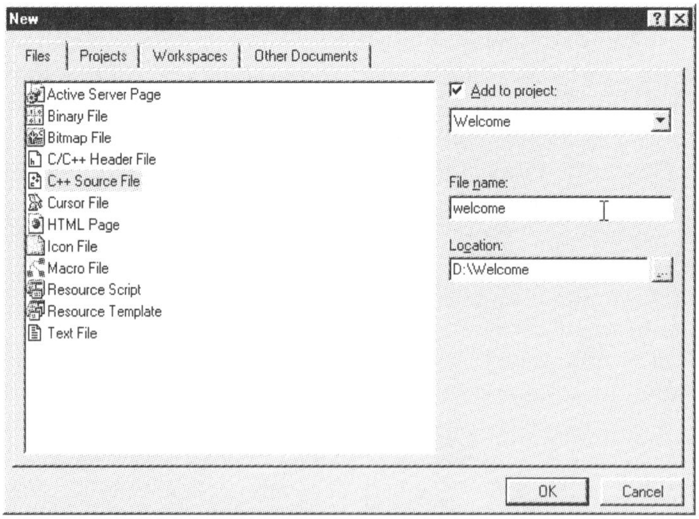

Fig. 1.8   **New** dialog displaying the **Files** tab.

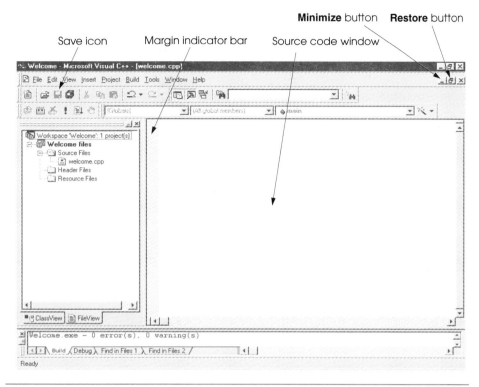

Fig. 1.9   IDE after adding a C++ source file.

The Visual C++ IDE has a highlighting scheme called *syntax coloring* for the keywords and comments in a C++ source file—you may have noticed this while you were typing the program. Syntax color highlighting is applied as you type your code and is applied to all source files opened in Visual C++. By default, keywords appear in blue, comments in green and other text in black, but you can set your own color preferences.

Testing and Debugging Tip 1.2

Visual C++'s syntax highlighting helps the programmer avoid using keywords accidentally as variable names. If a name appears blue (or whatever color you have selected for keywords), it is a keyword and you should not use it as a variable name or other identifier.

Another useful editor feature is *IntelliSense®*. When typing certain language elements, *IntelliSense* displays help automatically to let the programmer select a symbol from a list of names that can appear in the current context in the program; this saves typing time as well as the time it might otherwise take the programmer to look up options.

Figure 1.10 shows two examples of *IntelliSense*. When function **srand**'s opening parenthesis is typed, Visual C++ automatically displays its function header as a tip. When the dot (**.**) operator is typed after **struct** variable **c**, a list appears containing the valid members.

Testing and Debugging Tip 1.3

IntelliSense helps the programmer type a correct program.

```
source.cpp *
#include <iostream.h>
#include <time.h>

int main()
{
    srand(|
            void srand (unsigned int)

    return 0;    I
}
```

```
source.cpp *
struct Card {
    char *face;
    char *suit;
    int position;
};

int main()
{
    Card c;    I

    c.
       face
       position
       suit
    }
```

Fig. 1.10   IntelliSense.

After you have typed the program, click **Save** (in the **File** menu) or click the save button (the one that resembles a floppy disk icon) on the tool bar to save the file.

Before executing a program, you must eliminate all *syntax errors* (also called *compilation errors*) and create an *executable file*. A syntax error indicates that code in the program violates the syntax (i.e., the grammatical rules) of C++.

To compile the C++ file into an executable, click the **Build** menu's **Build welcome.exe** command or press the *F7 key*. Compiler messages and errors appear in the output pane's **Build** tab Fig. 1.11). If there are no errors when compilation is complete, **welcome.exe - 0 error(s), 0 warning(s)** should appear at the bottom of the output pane's **Build** tab as shown in Fig. 1.11 (this is sometimes called the "happy window").

If an error message appears in the output pane's **Build** tab, double-clicking anywhere on the error message displays the source file and places a *blue arrow marker* in the *margin indicator bar* (i.e., the gray strip to the left of the source code), indicating the offending line as shown in Fig. 1.12. The error in this particular case is a missing **<** character after **cout**.

Error messages are often longer than the output pane's width. The complete error message can be viewed either by using the horizontal scrollbar to the right of the tabs at the bottom of the screen (e.g. **Build**, **Debug**) or by reading the *status pane*. The status pane displays only the selected error message.

If you do not understand the error message, highlight the error message number by dragging the mouse over the number, then pressing the *F1 key*. This displays a help file that provides information about the error and some helpful hints as to the cause of the error. Please keep in mind that C++ compilers may mark a line as having an error when, in fact, the error occurs on a previous line of code.

```
--------------------Configuration: Welcome - Win32 Debug--------------------
Compiling...
welcome.cpp
Linking...

Welcome.exe - 0 error(s), 0 warning(s)
   Build  Debug  Find in Files 1  Find in Files 2
Ready                                                      Ln 8, Col 1   REC COL OVR READ
```

Fig. 1.11   **Output** pane showing a successful build.

Horizontal scrollbar to view long error messages   Insert/Remove Breakpoint

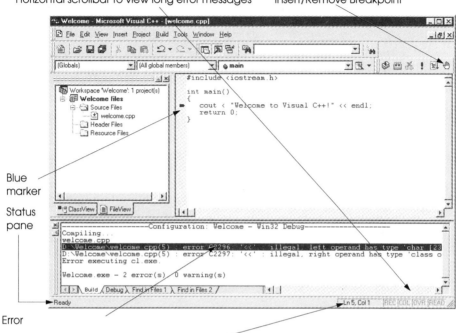

Blue
marker

Status
pane

Error

Line number and column number for the cursor are displayed here

Fig. 1.12   Blue marker indicating that a line contains a syntax error.

After fixing the error(s), recompile the program. C++ compilers often list more errors than actually occur in the program. For example, a C++ compiler may locate a syntax error in your program (e.g., a missing semicolon). That error may cause the compiler to report other errors in the program when, in fact, there may not be any other errors.

Testing and Debugging Tip 1.4

When a syntax error on a particular line is reported by the compiler, check that line for the syntax error. If the error is not on that line, check the preceding few lines of code for the cause of the syntax error.

Testing and Debugging Tip 1.5

After fixing one error, recompile your program. You may observe that the number of overall errors perceived by the compiler is significantly reduced.

Once the program compiles without errors, you can execute the program by clicking **Execute welcome.exe** in the **Build** menu. If you are using the *Visual C++ 6 Introductory Edition* software, a dialog is displayed containing the message

Note: The terms of the End User License Agreement for Visual C++ Introductory Edition do not permit redistribution of executables you create with this product.

each time a program is executed (users of the *Standard*, *Professional* and *Enterprise Editions* of Visual C++ 6 will not see this message). The program is executed in an MS-DOS window as shown in Fig. 1.13. Pressing any key closes the MS-DOS window.

Fig. 1.13   C++ program executing in an MS-DOS window.

To create another application, you follow the same steps outlined in this section using a different project name and directory. Before starting a new project you should close the current project by selecting the **File** menu's *Close Workspace* option. If a dialog appears asking if all document windows should be closed or if a file should be saved, click **Yes**. You are now ready to create a new project for your next application or open an existing project. To open an existing project, in the **File** menu you can select the **Recent Workspaces** option to select a recent workspace or you can select **Open...** to see an **Open Workspace** dialog and select a workspace (**.dsw** file) to open.

1.5 Debugger

The Visual C++ IDE provides a *debugger* tool to help the programmer find run-time logic errors in programs that compile and link successfully but do not produce expected results. The debugger lets the programmer view the executing program and its data as the programmer runs either one step at a time or at full speed. The program stops on a selected line of code or upon a fatal run-time error. When the programmer does not understand how incorrect results are produced by a program, running the program one statement at a time and monitoring the intermediate results can help the programmer isolate the cause of the error. The programmer can correct the code. The code example used in the screen captures is provided as **Examples/Ch01/Fig01_18**.

To use the debugger, set one or more *breakpoints*. A breakpoint is a marker set at a specified line of code that causes the debugger to suspend execution of the program upon reaching that line of code. Breakpoints help the programmer verify that a program is executing correctly. A breakpoint is set by clicking the line in the program where the breakpoint is to be placed and clicking the *Insert/Remove Breakpoint* button in the build toolbar (Fig. 1.12). The **Insert/Remove Breakpoint** button is grayed (disabled) unless the C++ code window is the active window (clicking in a window makes it active). When a breakpoint is set, a solid red circle appears in the margin indicator bar to the left of the line (Fig. 1.14). Breakpoints are removed by clicking the line with the breakpoint and clicking the **Insert/Remove Breakpoint** button or pressing the *F9 key*.

Selecting the *Go* command (in the **Build** menu's *Start Debug* submenu) starts the debugging process. Because we have chosen to debug a console application, the console window (i.e., MS-DOS window) that contains our application appears (Fig. 1.15). All program interaction (input and output) is performed in this window. Program execution suspends for input and at breakpoints. You may need to manually switch between the IDE and the console window to perform input. To switch between windows you can use *Alt + Tab* or click your program's panel on the Windows taskbar at the bottom of the screen.

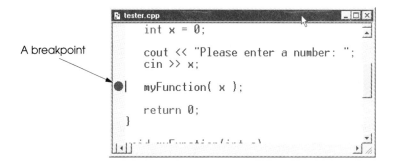

A breakpoint

Fig. 1.14 A breakpoint.

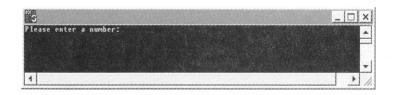

Fig. 1.15 C++ program executing in an MS-DOS window during debug mode.

Figure 1.16 shows program execution suspended at a breakpoint. The *yellow arrow* to the left of the statement

```
myFunction( x );
```

indicates that execution is suspended at this line. This statement will be the next statement executed. Note in the IDE that the **Build** menu is replaced with the **Debug** menu and that the title bar displays **[break]** to indicate that the IDE is in *debug mode*.

Testing and Debugging Tip 1.6

*Loops that iterate many times can be executed in full (without stopping every time through the loop) by placing a breakpoint after the loop and selecting **Go** from the **Debug** menu.*

The bottom portion of the IDE is divided into two windows—the **Variables** window (i.e., the left window) and the **Watch** window (i.e., the right window). The **Variables** window contains a list of the program's variables. Note that different variables can be viewed at different times, by clicking either the **Auto**, **Locals** or **this** tabs. The **Auto** tab displays the name and value of the variables or objects (discussed in Chapter 6 of *C++ How To Program: Second Edition*) used in both the previous statement and the current statement. The **Locals** tab displays the name and current value for all the local variables or objects in the current function's scope. The **this** tab displays data for the object to which the executing function belongs.

The variable values listed in the **Variables** window can be modified by the user for testing purposes. To modify a variable's value, click the **Value** *field* and enter a new value. Any modified value is colored red to indicate that it was changed during the debugging session by the programmer.

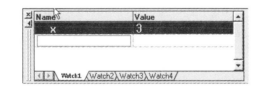

Fig. 1.16   Execution suspended at a breakpoint.

Often certain variables are monitored by the programmer during the debugging process—a process known as *setting a watch*. The **Watch** window allows the user to watch variables as their values change. Changes are displayed in the **Watch** window.

Variables can be typed directly into the **Watch** window or dragged with the mouse from either the **Variables** window or the source code window and dropped into the **Watch** window. A variable can be deleted from the **Watch** window by selecting the variable name and pressing the *Delete* key. The four tabs at the bottom of the **Watch** window are used by the programmer to group variables. Figure 1.17 shows a watch that has been set for variable **x**.

Like the **Variables** window, variable values can be modified in the **Watch** window by editing the **Value** field. Changed values are colored red. Note also that the current value of a variable during debugging can also be viewed by resting the mouse cursor over the name of that variable in the source code window (Fig. 1.18).

Fig. 1.17   **Watch** window showing the current value for variable **x**.

```
tester.cpp                              _ □ ×
int main()
{
    int x = 0;

    cout << "Please enter a number: ";
    cin >> x;

    myFunction( x );
                    x = 8

    return 0;|
```

Fig. 1.18   Displaying a variable's value using the mouse pointer.

The **Debug** toolbar contains buttons that control the debugging process. These buttons perform the same actions as the **Debug** menu items. Each button is labeled in Fig. 1.19. The **Debug** toolbar can be displayed by positioning the mouse pointer over an empty region of the main menu or any toolbar, right-clicking the mouse and selecting the **Debug** option in the popup menu.

The *Restart* button restarts the application, stopping at the beginning of the program to allow the programmer to set breakpoints before starting to execute the code. The *Stop Debugging* button ends the debugging session to let the programmer edit and rebuild the program before running another test.

Break Execution suspends program execution at the current location. *Apply Code Changes* allows the programmer to modify the source code while in debug mode. [Refer to the on-line documentation for limitations on this feature.] **Show Next Statement** places the cursor on the same line as the yellow arrow that indicates the next statement to execute. *Show Next Statement* is useful to reposition the cursor to the same line as the yellow arrow when editing the source code during debugging.

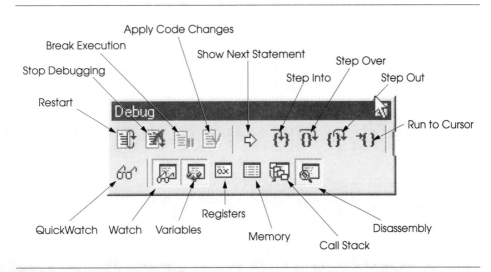

Fig. 1.19   **Debug** toolbar buttons.

The **Step Into** button executes program statements, one per click, including code in functions that are called, allowing the programmer to confirm the proper execution of the function, line-by-line. The results of the "step into" operation are shown in Fig. 1.20. Functions that can be stepped into include programmer-defined functions and C++ library functions. If you want to step into a C++ library function, Visual C++ may ask you to specify the location of that library.

Testing and Debugging Tip 1.7

The debugger allows you to "step into" a C++ library function to see how it uses your function call arguments to produce the value returned to your program.

The **Step Over** button executes the next executable line of code and advances the yellow arrow to the following executable line in the program. If the line of code contains a function call, the function is executed in its entirety as one step. This allows the user to execute the program one line at a time and examine the execution of the program without seeing the details of every function that is called. This is especially useful at `cin` and `cout` statements.

The **Step Out** button allows the user to step out of the current function and return control back to the line that called the function. If you **Step In** to a function that you do not need to examine, click **Step Out** to return to the caller.

Click the mouse on a line of code after a number of lines of code you do not wish to step through, then click the **Run to Cursor** button to execute all code up to the line where the cursor is positioned. This technique is useful for executing loops or functions without having to enter the loop or function.

Testing and Debugging Tip 1.8

*Loops that iterate many times can be executed in full by placing the cursor after the loop in the source code window and clicking the **Run to Cursor** button.*

Testing and Debugging Tip 1.9

*If you accidently step into a C++ library function, click **Step Out** to return to your code.*

```
tester.cpp

    return 0;
}

void myFunction(int c)
{
    if ( c > 0 )
        cout << "positive";
    else
        cout << "negative";
```

Fig. 1.20   Results of "stepping into" a function.

The *QuickWatch* button displays the *QuickWatch* *dialog* (Fig. 1.21), which is useful for monitoring expression values and variable values. The **QuickWatch** dialog provides a "snapshot" of one or more variable values at a point in time during the program's execution. To watch a variable, enter the variable name or expression into the *Expression* field and press *Enter*. As with the **Variables** window and **Watch** window, values can be edited in the **Value** field, but changed values are not color coded red. Clicking *Recalculate* is the same as pressing *Enter*.

To maintain a longer watch, click the *Add Watch* button to add the variable to the **Watch** window. When the **QuickWatch** dialog is dismissed by clicking **Close**, variables in the dialog are not preserved. The next time the **QuickWatch** dialog is displayed, the *Name* and *Value* fields are empty. The **QuickWatch** window can also be used to evaluate expressions such as arithmetic calculations (e.g., **a + b - 9**, etc.) and variable assignments (e.g., **x = 20**, etc.) by typing the expression into the **Expression** field.

The *Watch* button displays the **Watch** window. The *Variables* button displays the **Variables** window.

The *Memory* button displays the **Memory** window and the *Registers* button displays the **Registers** window (these buttons are beyond the scope of this book).

The *Call Stack* button displays a window containing the program's *function call stack*. A function call stack is a list of the functions that were called to get to the current line in the program. This helps the programmer see the flow of control that led to the current function being called. An alternative way of viewing the call stack is the **Context:** combo box (Fig. 1.16).

The *Disassembly* button displays the **Disassembly** window (Fig. 1.16). Analyzing a program that has been disassembled is a complex process likely to be used by only the most advanced programmers. We do not discuss the **Disassembly** window in this book.

Each of the buttons (e.g., **Variables, Watch, Memory, Registers, Call Stack** and **Disassembly**) act as *toggle buttons*—clicking them hides the window (if it is visible) or displays the window (if it is invisible). Debug windows (e.g., **Variables**, etc.) can also be displayed during the debugging session by selecting the appropriate debug window from the **View** menu's submenu *Debug Windows*.

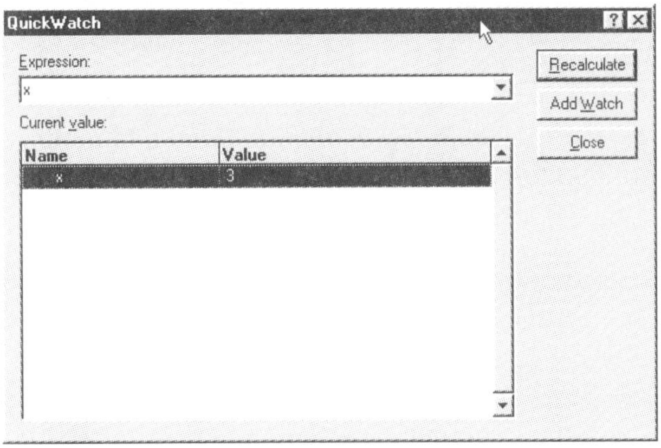

Fig. 1.21   **QuickWatch** dialog.

When a project is closed and reopened, any breakpoints set during a previous debugging session are still set. Breakpoints are persistent. You can gather information about breakpoints by selecting the **Edit** menu's *Breakpoints* menu item. When selected, the **Breakpoints** menu item displays the *Breakpoints* dialog (Fig. 1.22).

The **Breakpoints** dialog displays all the breakpoints currently set for the program. A checkbox appears next to each breakpoint. If the breakpoint is *active*, the checkbox contains a check. If the breakpoint is *disabled*, the checkbox is empty. A disabled breakpoint will not cause the debugger to stop but may be re-enabled at a later time. Clicking the checkbox allows the user to toggle the breakpoint *on* (checked) or *off* (unchecked). Additional breakpoints can be added by entering the desired line number into the *Break at* field. Note that when entering the line number in the *Break at* field, precede the line number with a period. For example, to set a breakpoint at line 13 we enter **.13** in the **Break at** field.

Visual C++ also allows breakpoints to be enabled when certain conditions are true. The programmer specifies the line number in the **Break at** field and presses the **Condition...** button to display the *Breakpoint Condition* dialog (first screen in Fig. 1.23). A condition is specified in the **Enter the expression to be evaluated** field and **OK** is pressed to set the condition. The second screen of Fig. 1.23 shows the **Breakpoints** dialog with the new breakpoint.

Figure 1.24 shows the debugging environment with a disabled breakpoint. Notice that the disabled breakpoint is still visible but it appears as a white circle. To make the breakpoint active, click the empty checkbox next to the breakpoint in the **Breakpoints** dialog.

Testing and Debugging Tip 1.10

Disabled breakpoints allow the programmer to maintain breakpoints in key locations in the program so they can be used again when needed. Disabled breakpoints are always visible.

Testing and Debugging Tip 1.11

When using the debugger to run a program at full speed, certain problems such as infinite loops can usually be interrupted by selecting **Break** *from the* **Debug** *menu.*

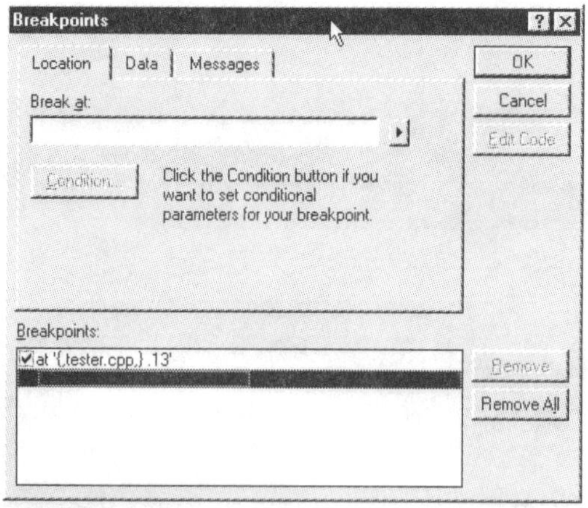

![Breakpoints dialog screenshot]

Fig. 1.22   Breakpoints dialog.

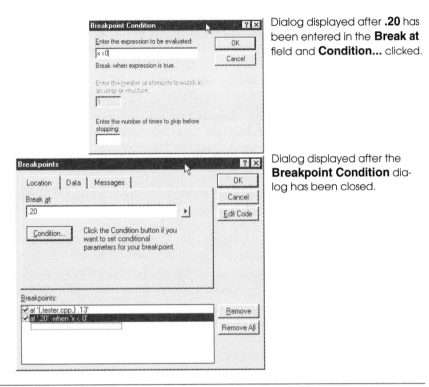

Dialog displayed after **.20** has been entered in the **Break at** field and **Condition...** clicked.

Dialog displayed after the **Breakpoint Condition** dialog has been closed.

Fig. 1.23   Adding a breakpoint to the **Breakpoints** dialog.

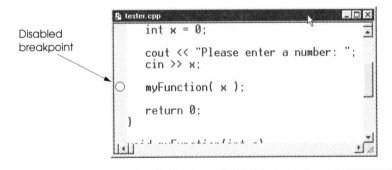

Disabled breakpoint

Fig. 1.24   A disabled breakpoint.

When you have finished your debugging session, click the ***Stop Debugging*** button on the **Debug** toolbar. The environment changes back to the pre-debugging setup. Refer to the on-line documentation for additional debugger features.

Summary

• The Microsoft Visual C++ integrated development environment (IDE) contains everything you need to create C++ programs—an editor (for typing and correcting your C++ programs), a compiler (for translating your C++ programs into machine language code), a debugger (for finding logic errors in your C++ programs after they are compiled) and much more.

- Visual C++ 6.0 uses the Microsoft Developer Network (MSDN) documentation, which is accessible by selecting **Contents** from the **Help** menu. The on-line documentation is also displayed by pressing *F1*. Placing the cursor on a line of code or error message and pressing *F1* displays context-sensitive help. Topics are displayed in tree-view format.

- The **MSDN Library Visual Studio 6.0** dialog's toolbar is used to navigate through on-line documentation in a similar manner to viewing pages in a Web browser.

- On-line information is divided into categories. Each category is preceded by a book icon. The **Visual C++ Start Page** is the starting point for an HTML-based approach to navigating the on-line documentation. The **Visual C++ Documentation Map** outlines the various sections of the Visual C++ documentation by category. The **What's New in Visual C++ 6.0** topic explains the newest features introduced in Visual C++ 6.0.

- Program files in Visual C++ are grouped into *projects*. A project is a text file that contains the name and location of all program files. Project files end with the **.dsp** extension. One or more projects are stored in a *workspace*. A workspace file has the **.dsw** extension.

- When executed, a **Win32 Console Application** receives input from an MS-DOS window and outputs data to the same MS-DOS window.

- The output pane displays various information, such as the status of compilation, syntax errors found by the compiler, undefined symbols, etc.

- The workspace pane contains two tabs, **ClassView** and **FileView**. **ClassView** allows classes, class members and functions to be viewed. **FileView** allows all project files to be viewed. **FileView** contains three folders: **Source Files**, **Header Files** and **Resource Files**.

- The Visual C++ IDE applies syntax highlighting on the program elements in a C++ source file. Syntax highlighting is applied as you type your code and is applied to all source files opened in Visual C++.

- You can customize the syntax color highlighting by selecting the **Options...** item from the **Tools** menu.

- *IntelliSense* displays context-sensitive lists of symbols from which the programmer can make a selection to help edit programs quickly and accurately.

- Before a program can be executed, all syntax errors (also called compilation errors) must be eliminated and an executable file must be created. A syntax error indicates that code in the program violates the syntax (grammatical) rules of C++.

- If an error message appears in the output pane's **Build** tab, double-clicking the error message results in the source code line being displayed, the edit caret being set on that line and a blue marker being placed in the margin indicator bar to identify the offending line. The error message is also displayed in the ouput pane.

- Highlighting an error message number, then pressing *F1* displays a help file that provides information about the error and some helpful hints as to what may have caused the error.

- The Visual C++ IDE provides a debugger for finding logic errors. A program must compile successfully before the debugger can be used. The debugger is a valuable tool for confirming that the application executes as expected.

- To use the debugger, one or more breakpoints may be set. Breakpoints are set by clicking the line in the program where program execution should temporarily pause and clicking the **Insert/Remove Breakpoint** button. When a breakpoint is set, a solid red circle appears in the margin indicator bar to the left of the line.

- Selecting the **Go** command (in the **Build** menu's **Start Debug** submenu) starts the debugging process.

- The bottom portion of the IDE is divided into two windows during debugging—the **Variables** window and the **Watch** window. The **Variables** window contains a list of the program's variables and their values. The **Watch** window allows the user to watch variables as they change.

- Variables can be typed directly into the **Watch** window or dragged and dropped into the **Watch** window from either the **Variables** window or the source code window. A variable can be deleted from the **Watch** window by selecting the variable name and pressing the *Delete* key. The four tabs at the bottom of the **Watch** window are used by the programmer to group variables.

- The **Debug** toolbar contains buttons that control the debugging process. These buttons perform the same actions as the **Debug** menu items.

- The **Restart** button restarts the program, stopping before the first executable statement.

- The **Stop Debugging** button ends the debugging session.

- **Break Execution** suspends program execution.

- **Apply Code Changes** allows the programmer to modify the source code while in debug mode.

- **Show Next Statement** is useful when editing the source code to reposition the cursor to the same line as the yellow arrow.

- The **Step Into** button allows functions to be stepped into—the user can confirm the proper execution of the function line-by-line.

- The **Step Over** button executes the next executable line of code and advances the yellow arrow to the next executable line in the program. If the line of code contains a function call, the function is executed in its entirety.

- The **Step Out** button allows the user to step out of the current function and return control back to the calling function.

- Click the **Run to Cursor** button to execute all code up to the line where the cursor is positioned.

- The **QuickWatch** button displays the **QuickWatch** dialog to get a "snapshot" of one or more variable values or expressions at a point in time during the program's execution. If the programmer wants to maintain a longer watch, the **Add Watch** button can be clicked to add the variable to the **Watch** window. Once the **QuickWatch** dialog is dismissed, variables in the dialog are not preserved.

- The **Variables** button displays/hides the **Variables** window.

- The **Watch** button displays/hides the **Watch** window.

- The **Call Stack** button displays/hides a window containing the program's function call stack. A function call stack is a list of the functions that were called to get to the current line in the program. You can also view the call stack through the **Context** combo box in the **Variables** window.

- Breakpoints are persistent. When a project is closed and reopened, any breakpoints set during a previous debugging session are still set.

- The **Breakpoints** dialog displays all the breakpoints currently set for the program. A checkbox appears next to each breakpoint. If the breakpoint is active, the checkbox contains a check. If the breakpoint is disabled, the checkbox is empty.

- Clicking the **Stop Debugging** button on the **Debug** toolbar ends a debugging session. The environment changes back to the program editing and building environment.

Terminology

Add Watch button in debugger	**Auto** tab
application	**Break Execution** button in debugger
Apply Code Changes button in debugger	breakpoint

Common Programming Error

1.1   Forgetting to add a C++ source file that is part of a program to the project for that program
prevents the program from compiling correctly.

Testing and Debugging Tips

1.1   Click in front of a brace (i.e., [or {) or a parenthesis (i.e., ()) and press **Ctrl +]** to find the
matching brace or parenthesis.

1.2   Visual C++'s syntax highlighting helps the programmer avoid using keywords accidentally as variable names. If a name appears blue (or whatever color you have selected for keywords), it is a keyword and you should not use it as a variable name or other identifier.

1.3   *IntelliSense* helps the programmer type a correct program.

1.4   When a syntax error on a particular line is reported by the compiler, check that line for the syntax error. If the error is not on that line, check the preceding few lines of code for the cause of the syntax error.

1.5   After fixing one error, recompile your program. You may observe that the number of overall errors perceived by the compiler is significantly reduced.

1.6   Loops that iterate many times can be executed in full (without stopping every time through the loop) by placing a breakpoint after the loop and selecting **Go** from the **Debug** menu.

1.7   The debugger allows you to "step into" a C++ library function to see how it uses your function call arguments to produce the value returned to your program.

1.8   Loops that iterate many times can be executed in full by placing the cursor after the loop in the source code window and clicking the **Run to Cursor** button.

1.9   If you accidently step into a C++ library function, click **Step Out** to return to your code.

1.10   Disabled breakpoints allow the programmer to maintain breakpoints in key locations in the program so they can be used again when needed. Disabled breakpoints are always visible.

1.11   When using the debugger to run a program at full speed, certain problems such as infinite loops can usually be interrupted by selecting **Break** from the **Debug** menu.

Self-Review Exercises

1.1   State whether each of the following is *true* or *false*. If *false*, explain why.
 a) The debugger is a syntax checker.
 b) Console applications receive their input from an MS-DOS window and output data to the same MS-DOS window.
 c) Pressing *F1* in the IDE loads and displays the on-line help.
 d) An enabled breakpoint appears as a white circle.
 e) Variable values displayed in the **Watch** window can be modified by the programmer during a debugging session.

1.2   Fill in the blanks for each of the following:
 a) _____ automatically displays function headers and lists members of a `class`, `struct` or `union`.
 b) The gray bar to the left of code in the source code window is the _____.
 c) The _____ window is used to watch variables.
 d) The _____ toolbar contains buttons that control the debugging process.
 e) Project files end with the _____ extension.

1.3   Fill in the blanks for each of the following:
 a) When clicked, the _____ button ends the debugging session.
 b) When clicked, the _____ button allows functions to be "stepped" into.
 c) When clicked, the _____ button allows the user to step out of the current function and return control back to the function call line.
 d) When clicked, the _____ button restarts the debugging session.
 e) When clicked, the _____ button executes the next executable line of code and advances the yellow arrow to the next executable line.

Answers to Self-Review Exercises

1.1   a) False. The debugger checks program logic. The compiler checks for syntax errors.
        b) True.
        c) True.
        d) False. An enabled breakpoint appears as a solid red circle. A disabled breakpoint appears as a white circle.
        e) True.

1.2   a) *IntelliSense*. b) margin indicator bar. c) **Watch**. d) **Debug**. e) **.dsp**.

1.3   a) **Stop Debugging**. b) **Step Into**. c) **Step Out**. d) **Restart**. e) **Step Over**.

Exercises

1.4   State whether each of the following is *true* or *false*. If *false*, explain why.
        a) Visual C++ allows breakpoints to be enabled when certain conditions are true.
        b) All source files must be part of a project before they can be compiled.
        c) Syntax errors must be eliminated before a program can be executed.
        d) Breakpoints are not persistent.
        e) When creating a **Win32 Console Application** project, a wizard is not employed.

1.5   Find the following terms in the on-line documentation **cin**, **cout**, **cerr**, **CWinApp**, **CFrameWnd**, **srand** and **setiosflags**.

1.6   (Prerequisite: *C++ How to Program: Second Edition,* Chapter 2 or equivalent control structure knowledge) Use the debugger to verify the flow of control for each of the following control structures: **while, do/while, for, if/else** and **switch**. Write your own program that uses each control structure and watch the yellow arrow move from statement to statement in the code.

1.7   (Prerequisite: *C++ How to Program: Second Edition,* Chapter 2, or equivalent control structure knowledge) Create a **Win32 Console Application** that prompts the user for a positive number and uses a repetition structure to print every even number less than the number input and greater than 0 in reverse order. For example, if the user enters **19**, the numbers **18**, **16**, **14**, **12**, **10**, **8**, **6**, **4** and **2** are printed.

1.8   (Prerequisite: *C++ How to Program: Second Edition,* Chapter 3 or equivalent function knowledge) Create a **Win32 Console Application** that prompts the user for an **int** and prints the sum and average of all the numbers less than or equal to the number and greater than zero. For example, if **10** is input, **55** is printed for the sum and **5.5** is printed for the average.

1.9   (Prerequisite: *C++ How to Program: Second Edition,* Chapter 4, or equivalent array knowledge) Create a **Win32 Console Application** that prompts the user for a series of **double** numbers, stores the numbers in a **double** array and prints the average, the results of rounding each element up to the next whole number, the results of rounding each element down to the next whole number and the largest value in the array.

1.10   (Prerequisite: *C++ How to Program: Second Edition,* Chapter 5, or equivalent pointer knowledge) Create a **Win32 Console Application** that prompts the user for a string, stores the string in a character array and uses pointers and pointer arithmetic to reverse the characters in the array. Use a separate function to perform the reverse operation. For example, if the user enters **hello**, the output should be **olleh**.

MFC Programming: Part I

Objectives

- To understand MFC classes and control flow.
- To understand event-driven programming.
- To understand the programmer's role in creating windows and responding to messages.
- To be able to create Win32 Applications.
- To be able to write simple MFC programs that have graphical user interfaces.
- To understand the resource definition language used to describe windows, controls and menus.
- To understand and use Hungarian notation to specify the type and scope of an identifier.
- To be able to create and use menus and dialogs.

The noblest function of an object is to be contemplated.
Miquel de Unamuno

An actor entering through the door, you've got nothing. But if he enters through the window, you've got a situation.
Billy Wilder

...The user should feel in control of the computer; not the other way around. This is achieved in applications that embody three qualities: responsiveness, permissiveness, and consistency.
Inside Macintosh, Volume 1
Apple Computer, Inc. 1985

A president is either constantly on top of events or. . . events will soon be on top of him.
Harry S. Truman

Outline

2.1 Introduction

In Chapter 1, you learned how to create Win32 console applications that executed in MS-DOS windows. The console applications did not have graphical elements (e.g., buttons, menus, etc.) that form a *graphical user interface* (*GUI*). Visual C++ enables the programmer to create Windows programs that have GUIs. In this chapter, we introduce some of the simpler *Microsoft Foundation Classes* (*MFC*) for creating Windows programs. In later chapters, we present more complex MFC classes.

Before studying this chapter, you should be familiar with C++ classes (Chapter 6 in *C++ How to Program: Second Edition*), inheritance (Chapter 9) and preprocessor directives such as **#define** for macros (Chapter 17).

2.2 MFC Classes

MFC is a class hierarchy a programmer can use to build Windows applications quickly and easily. Figure 2.1 lists a subset of the MFC hierarchy. You can view the complete MFC hierarchy by using the Visual C++ help facility to display the topic "Hierarchy Chart." Classes in Fig. 2.1 marked with an asterisk are not discussed in this book. MFC implements common characteristics of windows in *base classes* for *derived classes* to *inherit*. A class encapsulates functions and data. When one class is derived from another, it inherits the functions and data of its base class. To emphasize inheritance relationships, we indent each derived class to the right of its base class. **CObject** is the base class from which all other MFC classes are derived. **CWnd** is the base class for all the window types and controls. **CWnd** implements the common windows functions and data so that other windows can inherit rather than reimplement those characteristics.

The three primary classes used throughout this book are **CDialog**, **CFrameWnd** and **CWinApp**. Classes **CDialog** and **CFrameWnd** encapsulate functionality for creating windows. Class **CWinApp** encapsulates the functionality for creating and executing Windows applications. Each program we create uses **CWinApp** and/or the **CDialog** class and the **CFrameWnd** class.

Class	Description
CObject*	MFC common base class.
CGdiObject*	Graphical device interface class.
CPen	Class used for drawing patterns and colors.
CBrush	Class that represents fill patterns and colors.
CFont	Font class.
CBitmap	Bitmap class.
CDC*	Device context base class.
CClientDC	Client area device context class.
CPaintDC	Painting area device context class.
CMenu	Menu class.
CCmdTarget*	Event-messages target base class.
CWnd*	Window base class.
CDialog	Dialog box window class.
CStatic	Static control class (for text labels next to controls).
CButton	Button control class.
CListBox	List box control class.
CComboBox	Combo box control class.
CEdit	Edit box control class.
CFrameWnd	Frame window class.
CWinThread*	Task thread base class.
CWinApp	Windows application class.

Fig. 2.1   MFC class hierarchy subset.

2.3 Messages

Typically, programmers use MFC to create Windows programs with GUIs. Users interact with GUI by *moving the mouse*, *clicking the mouse*, *double-clicking the mouse*, *clicking a button*, *pressing a key*, etc. When a *GUI event* occurs, the Windows operating system sends a *message* to the program. Programming the functions that respond to these messages is called *event-driven programming*.

Software Engineering Observation 2.1

Messages can be generated by user actions, by other applications and by the operating system.

With event-driven programs, the user, not the programmer, dictates the order of program execution by interacting with the GUI. Instead of the program "driving" the user, the user "drives" the program. With the user in control, programs become more *user-friendly*. Consider, for example, a Web browser (e.g., *Microsoft Internet Explorer* or *Netscape Navigator*). When opened, the Web browser loads an initial page, then waits for the user to decide what to do next. The browser stays in this *event monitoring* state listening for *mes-*

sages indefinitely. If the user clicks a browser button, the browser performs some action. When the action is completed, the browser returns to its event-monitoring state.

MFC simplifies event-driven programming by providing an *application framework*— code that insulates the programmer from many of the details of Windows programming by providing an a convenient easy-to-use object-oriented interface to Windows.

In Windows, each message is identified by a unique number called a *message identifier*. Functions that execute in response to messages are called *message handlers*. Message identifiers are "tied to" message handlers by the *message map*. So when a program receives a message, the application framework looks up the message identifier in the Windows message map and calls the appropriate message handler. MFC programs that handle messages must declare the message map by using the **DECLARE_MESSAGE_MAP()** *macro* in the class declaration. A macro is a preprocessor statement that performs text substitution. (See Section 17.4 in *C++ How to Program: Second Edition* for a discussion of macros.)

Common Programming Error 2.1

Forgetting to use the **DECLARE_MESSAGE_MAP()** *macro is a nonfatal logic error. Objects created from the class will not receive messages, so although your program may execute, it is likely to produce incorrect results.*

The message map in the source file (**.cpp** file) begins with the line

    BEGIN_MESSAGE_MAP(*owner-class name*, *base-class name*)

and ends with the line

    END_MESSAGE_MAP()

Between these lines, the programmer "ties" message identifiers to message handlers with *message macros*. These message macros indicate the messages the program will handle. The programmer is responsible for placing the appropriate message macros in the message map. We discuss the *owner-class name* and the *base-class name* later in the chapter. We will say more about message macros momentarily.

Common Programming Error 2.2

Forgetting to add a message macro is a nonfatal logic error. The expected message handler will not be called. Your program may execute but produce incorrect results.

Windows predefines many common message identifiers. For example, **WM_PAINT** is the Windows-defined message identifier for the *paint message* (i.e., the message that draws the window on the screen). Programmers can also define their own message identifiers.

Software Engineering Observation 2.2

Predefined MFC message identifiers are located in header file **<afxwin.h>** *and have values in the range 0 through 1023. Programmer-defined message identifiers have values in the range 1024 through 65535.*

Message handlers are functions MFC calls to respond to messages passed to the program by Windows. Message handlers are mapped to message identifiers by the message map.

Predefined message identifiers have corresponding predefined message macros with similar names. For example, Windows message identifier **WM_PAINT** corresponds to MFC-defined message macro **ON_WM_PAINT()**. MFC-defined message macros have the same name as the message identifier—prefixed with "**ON_**" and are terminated with parentheses. MFC programmers use the macro **ON_COMMAND** to associate a message identifier with a programmer-defined message handler. Message-handler functions implement application-specific behavior.

2.4 MFC Resources

Rather than require the programmer to call functions to create GUI *controls* (i.e., buttons, etc.). Visual C++ provides a *resource definition language* to specify each GUI control's location, size, message identifier, etc. These resource definition language statements are stored in a *resource file* in the project directory. Resource files are identified by the **.rc** file extension.

Software Engineering Observation 2.3

Resource files contain resource definition language statements, rather than C++ source code statements.

The programmer can manually create and edit the application's **.rc** file as text, or use the IDE's *resource editor* to create and edit the resource file *graphically* by clicking-and-dragging the mouse. The *resource compiler* reads the resource file and translates the resource definition language statements into *object code* (i.e., machine language code) which is then linked with the application. During a build, the IDE executes the resource compiler. Resource files can use the C++ preprocessor to include files to resolve symbols such as message identifiers. We use resource files to create menus in Fig. 2.11.

2.5 Hungarian Notation

Typically, MFC programmers prefix variable names with letters indicating the variable's data type and scope. This *naming convention* is commonly referred to as *Hungarian notation*. In Fig. 2.2, we list some common Hungarian notation prefixes.

Good Programming Practice 2.1

Using Hungarian notation promotes software readability by providing type and scope information about each variable's name.

For example, a class that stores shape objects would typically be named **CShape**. The prefix **C** identifies **CShape** as a class. Prefixes can be combined in a declaration such as

```
double m_dSomeVariable;
```

which indicates that **m_dSomeVariable** has class scope because it is prefixed with **m_** and is a **double** because it is prefixed with **d**.

Software Engineering Observation 2.4

Hungarian notation is useful for distinguishing related variable names. For example, CRocket is a class and pCRocket is a pointer to a CRocket.

Software Engineering Observation 2.5

Hungarian notation is controversial—placing in a name a prefix that indicates the data type violates data abstraction and information hiding. Yet it can make a complex MFC C++ program easier to read.

Prefix	Description
ar	Array
b	**BOOL** (**int**) or **bool**
c	**char**
C	**class**
d	**double**
l	**long**
lp	**long** pointer
m_	**class** member variable
n or **i**	Integer
p	Pointer
s	String
sz	String with null termination
s_	**static class** member variable

Fig. 2.2   Common Hungarian notation prefixes used by MFC programmers.

Common Programming Error 2.3

Like any class library, MFC evolves over time. As a result, some MFC variables no longer have the same data type indicated by their Hungarian notation prefixes. This can lead to subtle programming errors.

2.6 Win32 Application Projects

In this section, we describe the steps necessary to create a ***Win32 Application*** project. This project type provides the basic framework for creating the example Windows programs we present in Chapters 2 through 5. The steps are similar to those outlined in Chapter 1 for creating a **Win32 Console Application**.

First, select **New** from the **File** menu to display the **New** dialog (Fig. 2.3). The **Projects** tab is selected by default (if not, click the **Projects** tab to select it). Select **Win32 Application**.

In the **Project name** field enter your project name. Click the *browse button* next to the **Location** field to specify the location on disk where the project will be saved. Click **OK** to close the dialog and display the **Win32 Application - Step 1 of 1** dialog (Fig. 2.4). Select **An empty project** to create a project that does not contain any files.

We describe how to create the files and write the code manually to demonstrate how to create a Windows application. Later, if you decide to use a *wizard* (i.e., a Visual C++ tool that creates project files and generates code), you will be able to understand what the wizard generates. We do not use wizards to create applications in this book because editing the code generated by wizards is not a task for beginning MFC programmers.

Click **Finish** to close the dialog and display the **New Project Information** dialog (Fig. 2.5). This dialog provides a summary of your project. Click **OK** to close the dialog.

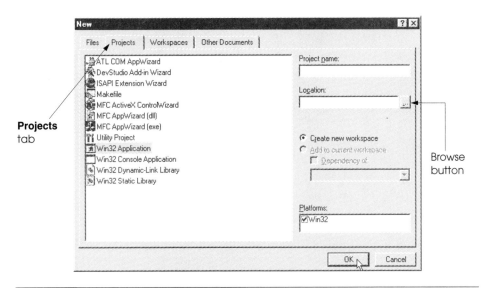

Fig. 2.3   New dialog displaying the **Projects** tab.

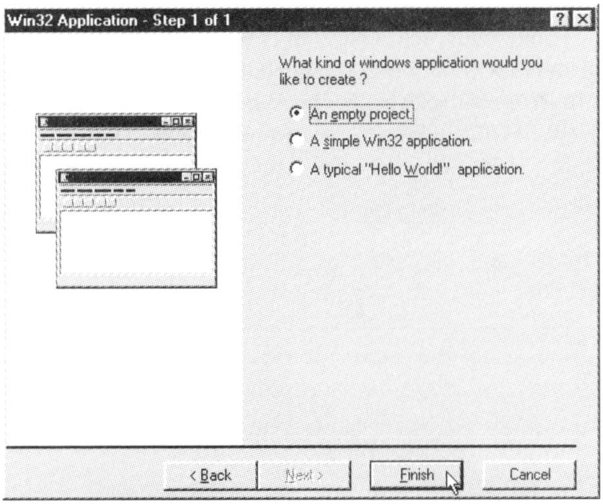

Fig. 2.4   Win32 Application - Step 1 of 1 dialog.

After creating an empty project, the next step is to add files to your project. You can create C++ *source files*, *header files* and *resource files*. Source files contain the code that implements the functions in your program. Header files contain common declarations that are typically shared by many files. Resource files contain definitions of menus, window layouts, etc. You will learn more about resource files later in the chapter.

Fig. 2.5   New Project Information dialog.

To create a C++ source file, select **New** from the **File** menu to display the **New** dialog (Fig. 2.6). The **Files** tab will be selected by default. Select **C++ Source File** and make sure that the **Add to Project** check box is checked. To create a header file, follow a similar procedure, except select **C/C++ Header File** in the **New** dialog. Fill in the **File name** and **Location** fields. Click **OK** to close the dialog and return to the Visual C++ IDE.

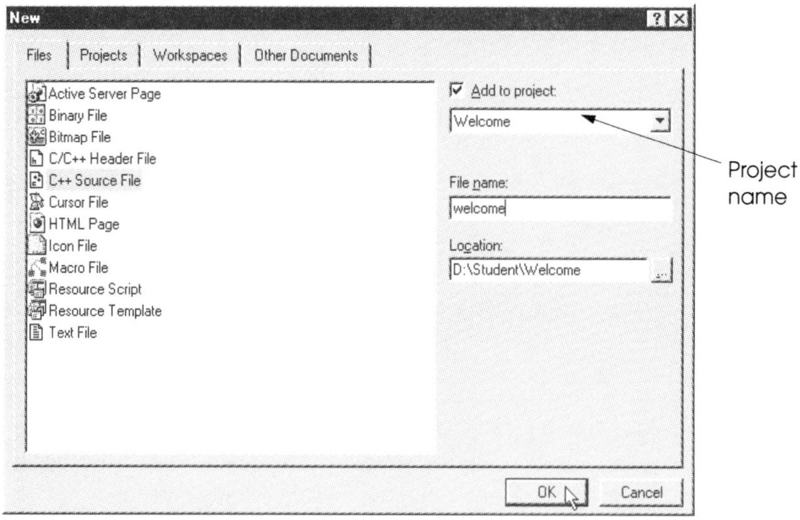

Fig. 2.6   New dialog displaying **Files** tab.

Several exercises in the book ask you to modify an example program or previous exercise. To add code from another file to the file you are editing, select the **Insert** menu item **File as text...,** find the file using the **Insert File** dialog, then click **OK.** This will copy the text to your edit window and will not change the input file. We use the project name **Welcome** and specify **D:\Student** for its location. The source file **welcome.cpp** will be created in the project directory **D:\Student\Welcome.** You may use whatever file name and project directory you want.

To minimize the size of the executable file and the build time, programmers typically use *dynamic linking*. The MFC *run-time functions* (preexisting MFC code that your program will call) are contained in a library (more specifically, a library accessed at run time called a *dynamic link library* or *DLL*) that is separate from the standard C++ run-time library. You do not have to know the name and location of the MFC library; you only have to tell Visual C++ that you want to link with the MFC library. Building a project means compiling the C++ source files and the resource files to produce object files, then linking the files to form an executable file. To set the options for building the project using MFC, select **Settings** from the **Project** menu to display the **Project Settings** dialog (Fig. 2.7). In order to use MFC, you must set up access to the library. In the **General** tab, select **Use MFC in a Shared DLL** in the **Microsoft Foundation Classes** combo box. This is the only option available besides the default **(none)** for the Visual C++ Introductory Edition software. Other versions of Visual C++ provide additional options. The preceding steps can be used to build the executable files for all the example programs.

Common Programming Error 2.4

Not setting the option **Use MFC in a Shared DLL** *for a* **Win32 Application** *causes a linker error when building MFC applications.*

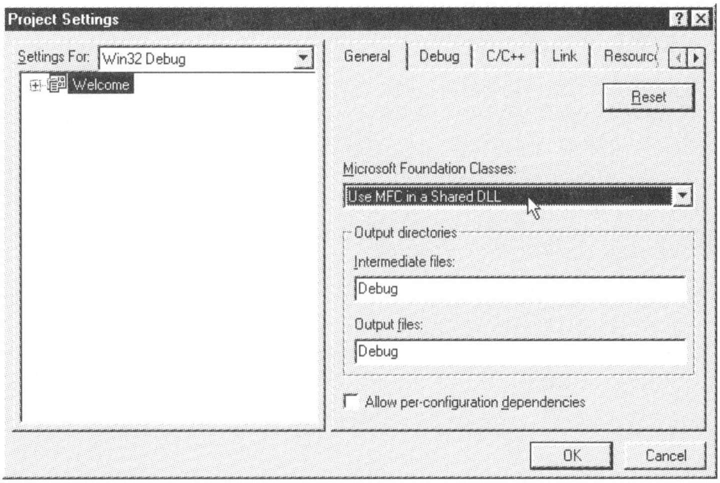

Fig. 2.7   Project Settings dialog.

2.7 Creating a Simple C++ Program with MFC

Next, we create our first program that displays the text "**Welcome to Visual C++ with MFC!**" in a window (Fig. 2.8). We introduce the minimum MFC code to create and display a control in a window. We explain each part of the program and its output window. The line numbers in the listings are not part of C++ or MFC; they are added here for reference purposes. All of the example programs in this book and in *C++ How to Program: Second Edition* are available via the "downloads" link at **www.deitel.com**. You may want to study the program code before reading the detailed walkthrough. This program has two files; **welcome.h** contains the interface and **welcome.cpp** contains the implementation.

```
1   // Fig. 2.8: welcome.h
2   // A First Program in C++ with MFC
3
4   class CWelcomeWindow : public CFrameWnd {
5   public:
6       CWelcomeWindow();      // constructor initializes window
7       ~CWelcomeWindow();     // destructor releases resources
8
9   private:
10      CStatic *m_pGreeting;     // contains welcome message
11  };
```

Fig. 2.8   A program that uses MFC to display text in a window (part 1 of 3).

```
12  // Fig. 2.8: welcome.cpp
13  // A First Program in C++ with MFC
14
15  // include application framework windows class definitions:
16  #include <afxwin.h>        // application frameworks header
17  #include "welcome.h"       // class definition for application
18
19  // constructor initializes the window
20  CWelcomeWindow::CWelcomeWindow()
21  {
22      // Create Window with Title Bar
23      Create( NULL,                    // default CFrameWnd class
24              "Welcome",               // window title
25              WS_OVERLAPPEDWINDOW,     // full-featured window
26              CRect( 100, 100, 300, 300 ) ); // screen coordinates
27
28      m_pGreeting = new CStatic;     // create a static control
29
30      m_pGreeting->Create(             // create Windows control
31          "Welcome to Visual C++ with MFC!", // text
32          WS_CHILD | WS_VISIBLE | WS_BORDER  // window styles
33          | SS_CENTER,                 // static object styles
34          CRect( 40, 50, 160, 100 ),   // window coordinates
35          this );                      // context that owns child window
36  }
```

Fig. 2.8   A program that uses MFC to display text in a window (part 2 of 3).

```
37
38   CWelcomeWindow::~CWelcomeWindow()
39   {
40      delete m_pGreeting;
41   }
42
43
44   // declare our application class based on CWinApp
45   class CWelcomeApp : public CWinApp {
46   public:
47      BOOL InitInstance()    // override default function
48      {
49         m_pMainWnd = new CWelcomeWindow();     // create window
50         m_pMainWnd->ShowWindow( m_nCmdShow );  // make visible
51         m_pMainWnd->UpdateWindow();            // force refresh
52         return TRUE;                           // report success
53      }
54
55   } welcomeApp;      // instantiate application
```

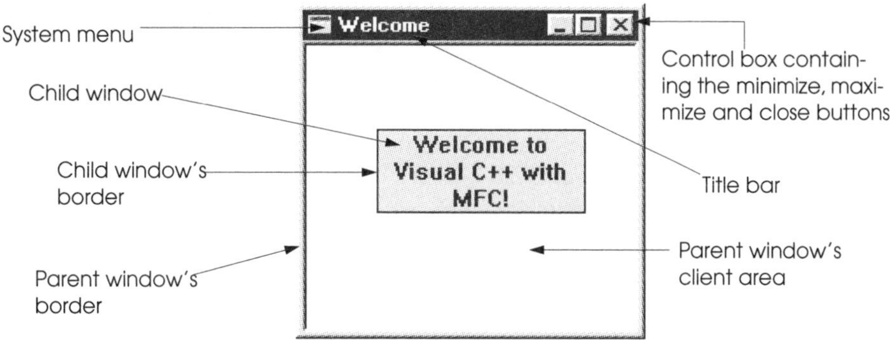

Fig. 2.8   A program that uses MFC to display text in a window (part 3 of 3).

Line 4

```
class CWelcomeWindow : public CFrameWnd {
```

begins the definition of class **CWelcomeWindow**. This programmer-defined class is derived from MFC class **CFrameWnd**, so class **CWelcomeWindow** inherits **CFrameWnd**'s *interface* and *implementation*. By inheriting from **CFrameWnd**, our class starts out with the basic windowing functionality we need for our application, such as the ability to move the window, resize the window, close the window, etc.

Lines 5 through 7

```
public:
   CWelcomeWindow();   // constructor initializes window
   ~CWelcomeWindow();  // destructor releases resources
```

define the **public** interface for this class to be only the constructor and the destructor for the **Welcome** window. Lines 9 and 10

```
private:
   CStatic *m_pGreeting;   // contains welcome message
```

define the **private** data for the class to be the pointer to the dynamically created control that will contain the greeting message. We will say more about the control type **CStatic** momentarily.

The preprocessor directives on lines 16 and 17

```
#include <afxwin.h>     // application frameworks header
#include "welcome.h"    // class definition for application
```

include the *application frameworks header* file **<afxwin.h>** and our own header file. The application frameworks header defines classes (e.g., **CFrameWnd**, **CWinApp**, etc.) and **include**s other header files such as **<afx.h>** that are required to create an MFC application. Application framework headers begin with the prefix "**afx**".

Common Programming Error 2.5

Not including **<afxwin.h>** *in an* **MFC Win32 Application** *program is a syntax error.*

Line 20

```
CWelcomeWindow::CWelcomeWindow()
```

begins the constructor definition. Constructors contain code for initializing an object of the class. A constructor always has the same name as the class, never **return**s a value and is executed automatically when an object of the class is created (or *instantiated*). Although this constructor does not take arguments—such a constructor is called a *default constructor*—constructors can take any number of arguments and can be overloaded.

So far, our **CWelcomeWindow** is only an MFC C++ object, it does not display anything on the screen. In order to do that, we must create the *main* or *top-level* window by calling function **Create**. The statement in lines 23 through 26

```
Create( NULL,                  // default CFrameWnd class
        "Welcome",             // window title
        WS_OVERLAPPEDWINDOW,   // full-featured window
        CRect( 100, 100, 300, 300 ) ); // screen coordinates
```

calls function **Create** (inherited from class **CFrameWnd**) to initialize our window. The first argument, **NULL**, indicates that we want to create a standard **CFrameWnd** window. The second argument, **"Welcome"**, is the name that will appear in the window's title bar. The third argument, *WS_OVERLAPPEDWINDOW*, indicates we want to create a window that can be resized. It will contain a system menu containing **Restore, Move, Size, Minimize, Maximize** and **Close** menu items and a title bar with a *control box* (containing the minimize, maximize and close buttons) on the right. The last argument creates a *CRect* object to store the window's pixel coordinates (Fig. 2.9). The arguments passed to **CRect** are coordinates (in pixels).

The first two **CRect** arguments (**100** and **100**) specify where the window's top-left corner is positioned on the screen. The last two values (**300** and **300**) are used to calculate the window's width and height. For this example, we want a window that is 200 pixels wide and 200 pixels high. To specify the width, take the *x*-coordinate (100) and add the desired width (200). The result of this addition is the coordinate 300 which is the third argument. The same process is used to determine the height.

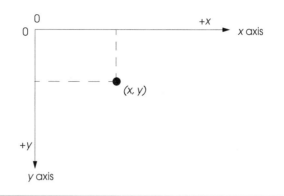

Fig. 2.9   Screen coordinate system.

Line 28

```
m_pGreeting = new CStatic;    // create a static control
```

creates a **new** MFC **CStatic** object (i.e. an object that displays text but does not send messages). This object is used for displaying the text **"Welcome to Visual C++ with MFC!"** This statement assigns the object's address to **m_pGreeting** (defined on line 10 as a **private CStatic** pointer). Remember, **private** members are not accessible to other classes. Operator **new** dynamically creates an object and returns its address, which the caller then stores in a pointer variable. To access a member function or data member of an object addressed by a pointer, we use the *arrow operator*, **->** (as in line 30).

Software Engineering Observation 2.6

*To ensure data integrity, make your data **private** and make your member functions **public**.*

After instantiating the MFC **CStatic** object, the statement on line 30

```
m_pGreeting->Create(            // create Windows control
   "Welcome to Visual C++ with MFC!", // text
   WS_CHILD | WS_VISIBLE | WS_BORDER  // window styles
   | SS_CENTER,                 // static object styles
   CRect( 40, 50, 160, 100 ),   // window coordinates
   this );                      // context that owns child window
```

creates the **CStatic** window (**CStatic** is derived from **CWnd**, the base class that implements common windows functions). The first argument sets the text message "**Welcome to Visual C++ with MFC!**" The second argument is a combination of four different constants that represent the characteristics that the **CStatic** window will have. The first style, **WS_CHILD**, indicates that the **CStatic** window is a *child window* (i.e., a window that is always contained inside another window). The second style, **WS_VISIBLE**, indicates that the **CStatic** window should be visible to the user. The third style, **WS_BORDER**, indicates that the **CStatic** window should have a border (e.g., the rectangle around the area displaying the text in Fig. 2.8). The last style, **SS_CENTER**, indicates that the text displayed in the **CStatic** window should be centered. These four constants are combined using the bit-wise inclusive or operator, **|**—this operator and bit manipulation in general are discussed in detail in Section 16.7 of *C++ How to Program: Second Edition*. The **CStatic** window coordinates are defined by the **CRect** object to be upper-left corner coordinate *(40, 50)* and size 160-by-100. Keyword *this* is the *owner* (i.e., the **CWelcomeWindow** object constructed on line 49) of the **CStatic** window (also called the *context* or *parent*). The owner contains the address of the **CStatic** child window and the **CStatic** child contains the address of its parent (i.e., the **CWelcomeWindow** object—**this**). The links between windows allow the Windows operating system to move and destroy a window and its contents as a group. For a discussion of the **this** pointer, see Section 7.5 in *C++ How to Program: Second Edition*. Line 38

```
CWelcomeWindow::~CWelcomeWindow()
```

begins the class's destructor definition. A destructor name is the name of its class prefixed with a *tilde*, **~**. Like constructors, destructors cannot **return** values. Unlike constructors, destructors cannot take arguments and, thus, cannot be overloaded. Destructors are automatically called when an object's resources are being released (i.e., deallocated). To prevent "memory leaks", a destructor for a class should explicitly **delete** any objects that were dynamically allocated with the **new** operator. The only resource **CWelcomeWindow** dynamically allocated is the **CStatic** object pointed to by **pGreeting**. Line 40

```
delete m_pGreeting;
```

deletes the **CStatic** object. Operator *delete* deallocates memory allocated by **new** after calling the object's destructor. Destruction completes the **CWelcomeWindow** object's life cycle.

The second class (i.e., **CWelcomeApp** on line 45) is derived from one of the most important MFC classes, *CWinApp*. Application start-up, execution and termination are controlled by **CWinApp**. Every MFC application has exactly one instance of a class derived from **CWinApp**. **CWelcomeApp** is an example of *"boilerplate" code*—a pattern of code that appears in multiple programs. This code replaces function **main**—the traditional entry point in a C++ program. Line 47

```
BOOL InitInstance()    // override default function
{
   m_pMainWnd = new CWelcomeWindow();     // create window
   m_pMainWnd->ShowWindow( m_nCmdShow ); // make visible
   m_pMainWnd->UpdateWindow();            // force refresh
   return TRUE;                           // report success
}
```

declares function *InitInstance*. This function starts the application by creating the top-level window. Function **InitInstance** creates a **CWelcomeWindow** object and causes it to run. The return type is MFC type *BOOL* (an integer used by MFC for boolean true and false values.)

On line 49 the **new** operator creates a **CWelcomeWindow** and stores its address in *m_pMainWnd*. This is a **public** data member of **CWelcomeApp** inherited from **CWinThread**. Function *ShowWindow* displays the window. Its argument, **m_nCmdShow**, is defined by base-class **CWinApp**. Variable **m_nCmdShow** is the main window's visibility option that is passed by Windows to the application to indicate whether the window is to be maximized when it is displayed. The first call to **ShowWindow** in a program can use **m_nCmdShow** as the argument so that Windows can determine the window placement. Function ***UpdateWindow*** forces the window to repaint itself. **InitInstance** returns **TRUE** to report successful completion.

Software Engineering Observation 2.7

*MFC function prototypes use **BOOL** (defined as **int**) rather than ANSI/ISO C++ data type **bool**. **BOOL** cannot be changed to **bool** without causing fatal diagnostics.*

Line 55

```
} welcomeApp;     // instantiate application
```

completes the definition of the **CWelcomeApp** and creates an instance of **CWelcomeApp** (i.e., an object) called **welcomeApp**. When **welcomeApp** is instantiated, its constructor and the constructors of all its base classes are called. Class **CWelcomeApp** does not provide a constructor, so the default constructor is called (see Chapter 9, "Inheritance," of *C++ How to Program: Second Edition*). The default constructor calls the base-class constructor (**CWinApp**), which stores the address of this object for ***WinMain*** (the main Windows entry point) to use. Function **WinMain** calls function **InitInstance** (line 47), which creates a **CWelcomeWindow**, which in turn creates a **CStatic** window (line 28) to display the text "**Welcome to Visual C++ with MFC!**". This execution sequence is the key to getting our welcome message window to appear. All of our other examples will contain similar code. The control flow in this example is shown in Fig. 2.10.

If you typed the code for this example or opened the project downloaded from **www.deitel.com**, you can now compile and execute the application. From the **Build** menu or tool bar, select **Build** (this compiles the program files). To execute the program, click the **Execute welcome.exe** menu item.

welcomeApp

CWinApp constructor
WinMain

InitInstance

new CWelcomeWindow

new CStatic

(line 55) Construction of **welcomeApp** calls the base-class constructor, **CWinApp**.

(implicit) **CWinApp** stores instance address. **WinMain** calls **InitInstance** (line 47).

InitInstance constructs the **CWelcomeWindow** object (line 49).

CWelcomeWindow constructs a **CStatic** object (line 28).

Fig. 2.10   Control flow for the program of Fig. 2.8.

2.8 Menus

Windows applications are often written to display groups of related selections called *menus* (see the screen images in Fig. 2.11). The selections provided depend on the application, but some—such as **Open** and **Save** in **File** menus—are common to most applications. Menus are an integral part of GUIs. When the user clicks a menu name, that menu expands to display its list of *menu items* from which the user makes a further selection by clicking a particular item. Visual C++ programmers use resources to add menus to application GUIs.

Software Engineering Observation 2.8

Menus (versus dialogs) simplify GUIs by reducing the number of controls the user sees.

Figure 2.11 creates a window containing four menus (**File**, **Entree**, **Beverage** and **Order**). When the user selects an item from the **Entree** or **Beverage** menu, the item's price is added to a running total, **m_dTotal** (line 47). The prices and the running total are stored internally and are not visible to the user. When the **Show Total** menu item is selected, a window is displayed with the total price of all the selected items. Eventually, the user selects **Exit** from the **File** menu to exit the application. The program adds the prices of the selected menu items. This program consists of four files, **CMenusWin.h** (containing the class definition), **menus.cpp** (containing the class' implementation), **menus.rc** (the resource file that defines our menus) and **menus_ids.h** (defines message identifiers).

```
1   // Fig. 2.11: CMenusWin.h
2   // create menus with MFC
3   const int TEXT_SIZE = 16;
4
5   class CMenusWin : public CFrameWnd {
6   public:
7      CMenusWin();
8      void tally( int &nCount, double dAmount );
9      afx_msg void OnExit();
10     afx_msg void OnDoFood(UINT nFood);
11     afx_msg void OnShowTotal();
12     afx_msg void OnClearTotal();
13
14  private:
15     int m_nChicken, m_nFish;     // count items ordered
16     int m_nGingerale, m_nRootbeer;
17     double m_dTotal;             // tally cost of the order
18
19     char m_szText[ TEXT_SIZE ];  // output string
20     ostrstream m_str;            // output string stream
21
22     DECLARE_MESSAGE_MAP()
23  };
```

Fig. 2.11   Creating and using menus (part 1 of 6).

```cpp
24  // Fig. 2.11: menus.cpp
25  // create menus with MFC
26  #include <afxwin.h>          // MFC application framework
27  #include <strstrea.h>        // string stream
28  #include <iomanip.h>         // I/O manipulators
29  #include "menus_ids.h"       // application message ID symbols
30  #include "CMenusWin.h"
31
32  CMenusWin::CMenusWin()                    // construct window
33     : m_str( m_szText, TEXT_SIZE )        // initialize ostrstream
34  {
35     Create( NULL, "Menus Example", WS_OVERLAPPEDWINDOW,
36        CRect( 0, 0, 200, 200 ), NULL, "Food" );
37
38     m_nChicken = m_nFish = 0;
39     m_nGingerale = m_nRootbeer = 0;
40     m_dTotal = 0.0;
41  }
42
43  // count each type of item ordered, compute total bill
44  void CMenusWin::tally( int &nCount, double dAmount )
45  {
46     nCount++;
47     m_dTotal += dAmount;
48  }
49
50  // afx_msg precedes each message handler function
51  afx_msg void CMenusWin::OnExit()
52  {
53     SendMessage( WM_CLOSE );
54  }
55
56  afx_msg void CMenusWin::OnDoFood(UINT nFood)
57  {
58     switch (nFood)
59     {
60     case IDM_CHICKEN:
61        tally( m_nChicken, 2.25 );
62        break;
63     case IDM_FISH:
64        tally( m_nFish, 1.80 );
65        break;
66     case IDM_GINGERALE:
67        tally( m_nGingerale, .80 );
68        break;
69     case IDM_ROOTBEER:
70        tally( m_nRootbeer, .80 );
71        break;
72     }
73  }
74
```

Fig. 2.11 Creating and using menus (part 2 of 6).

```
75   afx_msg void CMenusWin::OnShowTotal()
76   {
77      m_str.seekp( 0 );                     // reset output string
78      m_str << setprecision( 2 )
79          << setiosflags( ios::fixed | ios::showpoint )
80          << "        $" << m_dTotal << ends;   // stopper
81
82      // display new dialog box with output string
83      MessageBox( m_szText, "Your total is:" );
84      m_dTotal = 0.0;
85   }
86
87   afx_msg void CMenusWin::OnClearTotal()
88   {
89      m_dTotal = 0.0;
90      MessageBox( "           $0.00", "Cleared Order" );
91   }
92
93   BEGIN_MESSAGE_MAP( CMenusWin, CFrameWnd )
94
95      ON_COMMAND( IDM_EXIT, OnExit )
96
97      ON_COMMAND_RANGE(IDM_CHICKEN, IDM_ROOTBEER, OnDoFood)
98
99      ON_COMMAND( IDM_SHOW_TOTAL, OnShowTotal )
100     ON_COMMAND( IDM_CLEAR_TOTAL, OnClearTotal )
101
102  END_MESSAGE_MAP()
103
104
105  class CMenusApp : public CWinApp {
106  public:
107     BOOL InitInstance()          // called by CWinApp::CWinApp
108     {
109        m_pMainWnd = new CMenusWin;          // create window
110        m_pMainWnd->ShowWindow( m_nCmdShow ); // make it visible
111        m_pMainWnd->UpdateWindow();          // force refresh
112        return TRUE;                          // report success
113     }
114
115  } menusApp;                     // calls CWinApp::CWinApp
```

Fig. 2.11   Creating and using menus (part 3 of 6).

In the **CMenusWin.h** file, lines 5 through 23 declare the class **CMenusWin** to be derived from **CFrameWnd** (**public** here means all **CFrameWnd public** functions are **public** to the users of this class). Lines 7 through 12 declare the **public** interface functions and lines 15 through 20 declare the **private** data members of the class.

Line 22 uses the macro **DECLARE_MESSAGE_MAP()** to declare a message map (i.e., a data structure that maps message identifiers to their respective message handler functions) to be a part of the **CMenusWin** class. An MFC window class must use this macro if it has a message map and message handler functions.

```
116  // Fig. 2.11:  menus_ids.h
117  // define messages used by menus.cpp and menus.rc
118  #define  IDM_EXIT          2000
119
120  #define  IDM_CHICKEN       2021
121  #define  IDM_FISH          2022
122
123  #define  IDM_GINGERALE     2041
124  #define  IDM_ROOTBEER      2042
125
126  #define  IDM_SHOW_TOTAL    2051
127  #define  IDM_CLEAR_TOTAL   2052
```

Fig. 2.11   Creating and using menus (part 4 of 6).

```
128  // Fig. 2.11    menus.rc
129  // resource script for menus example
130  #include <afxres.h>
131  #include "menus_ids.h"
132
133  Food MENU
134  {
135     POPUP "File"
136     {
137        MENUITEM "Exit", IDM_EXIT
138     }
139
140     POPUP "Entree"
141     {
142        MENUITEM "Chicken", IDM_CHICKEN
143        MENUITEM "Fish", IDM_FISH
144     }
145
146     POPUP "Beverage"
147     {
148        MENUITEM "Ginger Ale", IDM_GINGERALE
149        MENUITEM "Root Beer", IDM_ROOTBEER
150     }
151
152     POPUP "Order"
153     {
154        MENUITEM "Show Total", IDM_SHOW_TOTAL
155        MENUITEM "Clear Total", IDM_CLEAR_TOTAL
156     }
157  }
```

Fig. 2.11   Creating and using menus (part 5 of 6).

In the **menus.cpp** file, the preprocessor directives on lines 27 and 28

```
#include <strstrea.h>
#include <iomanip.h>
```

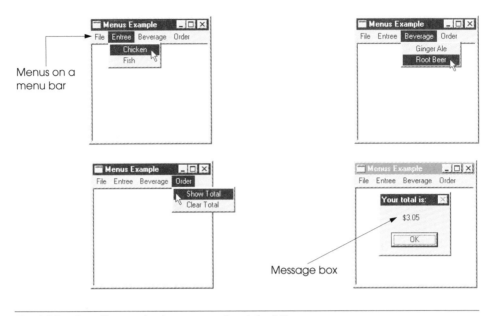

Fig. 2.11 Creating and using menus (part 6 of 6).

include the string stream class header and bring in the function prototypes that enable us to use parameterized manipulators such as **setprecision(2)** in line 78. This program demonstrates using a string stream (i.e., **ostrstream**) to convert and format floating-point values for display in a window. Using class **ostrstream** is similar to using **cout**. Because we are creating a Windows application, we do not use **cout** to display characters or **cin** to read characters from the keyboard. Object **cout** is for use with Windows console applications (i.e., the types of applications created in Chapter 1 and throughout *C++ How to Program: Second Edition*).

The preprocessor directive on line 29

```
#include "menus_ids.h"
```

includes our programmer-defined header file **menus_ids.h** (lines 116 through 127). In this header, we define our message identifiers for the menus which are used in both our C++ module and our resource file. These message identifiers allow the message dispatcher to call the appropriate message handler when a menu item is selected.

Line 30

```
#include "CMenusWin.h"
```

includes the class definition file for this application.

The **CMenusWin** constructor (line 32) constructs our **ostrstream** class member object **m_str** (line 20). The first argument passed to the **ostrstream** constructor is the address of the character array (**m_szText** declared on line 19) where characters sent to **m_str** by the stream insertion operator, **<<**, are stored. The second argument (**TEXT_SIZE** defined on line 3) is the array length of the first argument—**m_szText**. When the **CMenusWin** constructor executes, constructors for the base classes and member objects execute. For simple conversions of variables to display text, a number of options are available. The **ostrstream** object used in this example requires a character array and the array's size.

Line 35

```
Create( NULL, "Menus Example", WS_OVERLAPPEDWINDOW,
        CRect( 0, 0, 200, 200 ), NULL, "Food" );
```

creates the application's window. The first argument to **Create**, is **NULL**, meaning to use the default window properties for this window. The second argument, **"Menus Example"**, is the text to display in the title bar. The third argument, **WS_OVERLAPPEDWINDOW**, is the window style "overlapped window." This is the typical main window style with menus, a title bar with an icon and caption on the left and **Minimize**, **Maximize** and **Close** buttons on the right. The fourth argument can specify the window's screen coordinates in a **CRect** object or the MFC-predefined **CRect** object, *rectDefault* can be given to allow Windows to choose the window size and position. The **CRect** given in this example specifies that the window will have its top-left corner at screen position *(0, 0)* and its bottom right corner will be inside the bounding location *(200, 200)*. This window is not a child window, so **NULL** is passed as the fifth argument. The final argument, **"Food"**, is the label on the **MENU** definition in the resource file (line 133) that associates the menus with this window.

Function **tally** (line 44) contains common code needed by the menu message handlers. Integer argument **nCount** is a reference (indicated by the **&** in the declaration) to the variable passed to this function (see Section 3.17, "References and Reference Parameters," in *C++ How to Program: Second Edition*). The variable referenced by **nCount** is incremented by one to keep a count of each item sold. Argument **dAmount** is a double-precision floating-point variable that contains the price of the selected food item. Variable **m_dTotal** (line 47) is the sum of all prices of items ordered. This program is a starting point for exercises that will use the output string stream in various functions for displaying information about orders.

The function on line 51

```
afx_msg void CMenusWin::OnExit()
{
    SendMessage( WM_CLOSE );
}
```

is the first message handler in our program. This prefix *afx_msg* is an MFC naming convention used to mark a message handler. The name **OnExit** follows the MFC naming convention of using **On** as the prefix to a message handler name. The name indicates that the function is called "on" (or upon) selection of the menu item **Exit**. The function takes no arguments and returns **void**. Line 53 calls **CWnd** class function *SendMessage* passing it the close message ID (*WM_CLOSE*) to terminate program execution. Message handler **OnClose** inherited from class **CWnd** receives the message, closes the window and terminates the program.

Good Programming Practice 2.2

*Prefixing message handler names with **On** allows message handlers to be easily identified.*

The message handler **OnDoFood** (line 56) receives a range of similar messages that the **switch** statement starting on line 58 decodes. A common message handler can process similar messages by using the message identifier in a **switch** or in a subscript expression. This is a useful technique for menu items and buttons that have the same behavior but have differing data. The keys 0 through 9 on a calculator are a typical example.

Line 61

```
tally( m_nChicken, 2.25 );
```

executes when the user selects the **Chicken** menu item. It calls function **tally** passing by reference the appropriate food-type counter (e.g., **m_nChicken**) and the food's price (e.g., **2.25**).

The message handler on line 75

```
afx_msg void CMenusWin::OnShowTotal()
{
   m_str.seekp( 0 );                    // reset output string
   m_str << setprecision( 2 )
         << setiosflags( ios::fixed | ios::showpoint )
         << "         $" << m_dTotal << ends;  // stopper

   // display new dialog box with output string
   MessageBox( m_szText, "Your total is:" );
   m_dTotal = 0.0;
}
```

executes when the user clicks menu **Show Total**. Data written to **m_szText** by **m_str** is appended (i.e., a pointer—called a *put pointer* is used behind the scenes by **m_str** to keep track of the subscript where the next write will occur). Function **seekp** (line 77) allows the programmer to control the position (i.e., subscript) of the put pointer. When passed zero, **seekp** positions the put pointer to the beginning of the array. Lines 78 through 80 format **m_dTotal** as a dollar amount. Stream manipulator **ends** places a null terminator character to mark the end of the string. Function **MessageBox** is called (line 83) to display the formatted characters stored in **m_szText** in a message box (i.e., the window labeled message box in Fig. 2.11).

Lines 93 through 102

```
BEGIN_MESSAGE_MAP( CMenusWin, CFrameWnd )

   ON_COMMAND( IDM_EXIT, OnExit )

   ON_COMMAND_RANGE( IDM_CHICKEN, IDM_ROOTBEER, OnDoFood )

   ON_COMMAND( IDM_SHOW_TOTAL, OnShowTotal )
   ON_COMMAND( IDM_CLEAR_TOTAL, OnClearTotal )

END_MESSAGE_MAP()
```

use macros to create the *message map*, which contains message identifiers and message handler addresses. We use **ON_COMMAND** and **ON_COMMAND_RANGE** macros to build message map entries for our application-specific messages and message handlers. The message identifier symbols use prefix **IDM_** (for "identifier of a menu") to follow MFC naming conventions. Message handler functions have the prefix **On** (e.g., **OnExit**) by convention. File **menus_ids.h** (lines 116) defines the message identifiers and their numeric values.

Good Programming Practice 2.3

*Beginning a message identifier with the prefix **IDM_** distinguishes it as an identifier for a menu.*

Good Programming Practice 2.4

*Insert a blank line between adjacent groups of **ON_COMMAND** macros to show the boundaries between pop-up menus.*

Resource file **menus.rc** (lines 128 through 157) defines the menu and associates the message identifiers with the menu items, providing the association between the program code and the window description. Resource files contain resource definition language (i.e., a language that describes GUI elements such as menus, windows, controls, etc.) statements. The resource definition language is not C++. The resource definition language is documented in the online help. Clicking a directive name or a keyword in a resource definition statement and pressing *F1* (i.e., the help key) causes the documentation to be displayed.

To create a resource file with the source code editor, click the **New Text File** icon (below the Visual C++ IDE **File** menu) and enter your resource definition language statements and save the file with the **.rc** extension. Next, select **Add to Project** from the **Project** menu and select **Files...**. Select your **.rc** file and click **OK.** When you open the resource file for text editing, use the **File** menu **Open** command and select **Text** in the **Open as:** combo box at the bottom of the **Open** dialog. [*Note*: Opening a resource file in the default mode (**Auto** in the **Open as:** combo box) or double-clicking the file name loads and displays the graphical resource editor—which is not discussed in this book.]

Lines 130 and 131

```
#include <afxres.h>
#include "menus_ids.h"
```

include the definitions of application framework predefined resources from MFC header file **<afxres.h>** and our menu message identifiers from **"menus_ids.h"**. The header file uses **#define** preprocessor directives (see Chapter 17, "The Preprocessor," in *C++ How to Program: Second Edition*) to associate message-control identifier symbols with their numeric values.

Common Programming Error 2.6

*Resource definitions can use **#define** preprocessor symbols. Attempting to use keyword **const** is a syntax error.*

Look-and-Feel Observation 2.1

*Most Windows applications provide a **File** menu as the left menu in the menu bar.*

Line 133

```
Food MENU
```

introduces the definition of our menus. The **MENU** directive name **Food** corresponds to the sixth argument in the call to function **Create** on line 35. Lines 135 through 138

```
POPUP "File"
{
    MENUITEM "Exit", IDM_EXIT
}
```

define a menu (i.e., **File**) with one menu item (i.e., **Exit**). Resource statement **POPUP** identifies a menu and its name **"File"** that will appear in the menu bar of the window. When clicked, the menu displays its list of menu items. **MENUITEM** specifies individual menu items. The menu item's name is **Exit** and the message it sends when selected is **IDM_EXIT** (defined in line 118).

The **MENUITEM** resource definition statement defines the name **"Exit"** and the message identifier for the menu item. When the user selects the menu item by clicking the mouse, Windows sends a message with the numeric value we associated (in line 118) with symbol **IDM_EXIT** to the application. The **menus_id.h** file contains the definitions for our message identifiers used by the **menus.rc** file and the **menus.cpp** file.

2.9 Dialog Boxes

Class **CDialog** is used to create windows called *dialog boxes*. Windows programs typically use dialog boxes to get information (e.g., passwords, file names, etc.,) that is input by the user. The user types information into the dialog box's fields and then typically clicks a button to input the information and close the dialog box.

Some application programs, such as a calculator, do not require all the features of a **CFrameWnd** window for the GUI. These applications can use a dialog box for the GUI. These types of programs are called *dialog-based programs*. In this section we develop a dialog-based program to add a series of numbers input by the user. The example introduces dialog boxes, *button controls* and *edit text controls* (also called *edit box* controls).

Figure 2.12 uses a dialog box containing two buttons and two edit text controls to prompt the user for a series of numbers. When the user enters a number in the white edit box and clicks **Add**, the number is added to a running total and displayed in the **Total:** edit box. This box is gray because it does not accept input from the user.

```
1   // Fig. 2.12: CAdditionDialog.h
2   // Addition program with MFC dialog box
3
4   class CAdditionDialog : public CDialog {
5   public:
6      CAdditionDialog()
7         : CDialog( "Addition" ), m_nTotal( 0 ) {}
8
9      afx_msg void OnAdd();          // clicked the "Add" button
10     afx_msg void OnClear();        // clicked the "Clear" button
11
12  private:
13     int m_nTotal;                  // sum of numbers
14
15     DECLARE_MESSAGE_MAP()
16  };
```

Fig. 2.12 A dialog-based application (part 1 of 6).

```
17   // Fig. 2.12: addition.cpp
18   // Addition program with MFC dialog box
19   #include <afxwin.h>
20   #include "addition_ids.h"
21   #include "CAdditionDialog.h"
22
23   // clicked the "Add" button
24   afx_msg void CAdditionDialog::OnAdd()
25   {
26      const TEXT_SIZE = 16;
27      char szText[ TEXT_SIZE + 1 ]; // buffer for conversions
28
29      // get addresses of Edit Box Controls
30
31      CEdit *pTotal = ( CEdit * ) ( GetDlgItem( IDC_TOTAL ) );
32      CEdit *pNum   = ( CEdit * ) ( GetDlgItem( IDC_NUMBER ) );
33
34      pNum->GetWindowText( szText, TEXT_SIZE ); // get Number
35      m_nTotal += atoi( szText );       // add binary value
36
37      itoa( m_nTotal, szText, 10 );     // convert total to text
38
39      pTotal->SetWindowText( szText ); // display total
40      pNum->SetWindowText( "" );        // clear input
41      pNum->SetFocus();                 // next input to Number
42   }
43
44   // clicked the "Clear" button
45   afx_msg void CAdditionDialog::OnClear()
46   {
47      CEdit *pTotal = ( CEdit * ) ( GetDlgItem( IDC_TOTAL ) );
48      CEdit *pNum   = ( CEdit * ) ( GetDlgItem( IDC_NUMBER ) );
49
50      m_nTotal = 0;                     // clear the total
51      pTotal->SetWindowText( "" ); // clear the edit box
52      pNum->SetFocus();                 // next input to Number
53   }
54
55   BEGIN_MESSAGE_MAP( CAdditionDialog, CDialog )
56      ON_COMMAND( IDC_ADD, OnAdd )
57      ON_COMMAND( IDC_CLEAR, OnClear )
58   END_MESSAGE_MAP()
59
```

Fig. 2.12 A dialog-based application (part 2 of 6).

Class **CAdditionDialog** (line 4) is derived from MFC class **CDialog**. The constructor is defined on line 6 and is invoked on line 65. The dialog resource name (i.e., **"Addition"**) is passed to the **CDialog** base-class constructor to initialize the dialog box with the attributes specified in the resource file (line 83). Instance variable **m_nTotal** is set to 0. The empty braces **{ }** indicate that no code needs to run in the **CAdditionDialog** constructor—all the initialization is specified in the initializer list (line 7).

```
60   // dialog-based application
61   class CAdditionApp : public CWinApp {
62   public:
63      BOOL InitInstance()
64      {
65         CAdditionDialog additionDialog;
66         additionDialog.DoModal();   // run dialog
67         return FALSE;               // finished
68      }
69
70   } addition;
```

Fig. 2.12   A dialog-based application (part 3 of 6).

```
71   // Fig 2.12: addition_ids.h
72   // Define Message Numbers
73
74   #define IDC_NUMBER 2000
75   #define IDC_ADD    2001
76   #define IDC_TOTAL  2002
77   #define IDC_CLEAR  2003
```

Fig. 2.12   A dialog-based application (part 4 of 6).

```
78   // Fig. 2.12: Addition.rc
79   // resource script for addition example
80   #include "afxres.h"
81   #include "addition_ids.h"
82
83   Addition DIALOG  50, 50, 130, 130
84   STYLE DS_MODALFRAME | WS_POPUP | WS_CAPTION | WS_SYSMENU
85
86   CAPTION "Addition Dialog Box"
87   {
88       LTEXT          "Enter a number:", IDC_STATIC, 30, 20, 50, 8
89       EDITTEXT       IDC_NUMBER, 30, 30, 72, 16, ES_NUMBER
90
91       DEFPUSHBUTTON "Add", IDC_ADD, 50, 50, 30, 15
92
93       LTEXT          "Total:", IDC_STATIC, 30, 70, 20, 8
94       EDITTEXT       IDC_TOTAL, 30, 80, 70, 16,
95                      ES_READONLY | NOT WS_TABSTOP
96
97       PUSHBUTTON     "Clear", IDC_CLEAR, 50, 100, 30, 15,
98                      NOT WS_TABSTOP
99   }
```

Fig. 2.12   A dialog-based application (part 5 of 6).

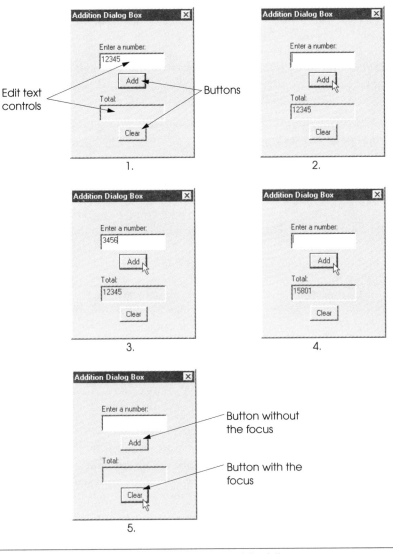

Fig. 2.12   A dialog-based application (part 6 of 6).

Message handler **OnAdd** (line 24) is called when the user clicks button **Add**. This message handler defines the **szText** character array to be 17 characters long. Lines 31 and 32

```
CEdit *pTotal = ( CEdit * )( GetDlgItem( IDC_TOTAL ) );
CEdit *pNum   = ( CEdit * )( GetDlgItem( IDC_NUMBER ) );
```

call *GetDlgItem* to retrieve the addresses of the two edit boxes in the dialog box so that we can manipulate them (i.e., read and write the contents) programmatically. The *ID codes* **IDC_TOTAL** and **IDC_NUMBER**—defined in header file **addition_ids.h** (lines 71 through 77) for the controls are used by *GetDlgItem* to get pointers to the edit texts.

Function **GetDlgItem** returns the addresses as base-class **CWnd** pointers. Because we are assigning a base-class pointer (**CWnd ***) to a derived-class pointer (**CEdit ***), we cast the pointer (see Chapter 9, "Inheritance," of *C++ How to Program: Second Edition*). The addresses returned by **GetDlgItem** can change from one message to another, because Windows reallocates memory as it creates and deletes windows. We must therefore call **GetDlgItem** in each invocation of the message handler.

Lines 34 and 35

```
pNum->GetWindowText( szText, TEXT_SIZE ); // get Number
m_nTotal += atoi( szText );               // add binary value
```

call **GetWindowText**, inherited from **CWnd**, to retrieve the text in the edit box control pointed to by **pNum** and copy the text to the **szText char** array, which is **TEXT_SIZE + 1** in length. The length corresponds to the size specified in the resource file for the edit box (discussed below). Line 35 converts the text in **szText** to an **int** value using **<stdlib.h>** function, *atoi*, and adds it to **m_nTotal**. The **stdlib.h** file is included by **<afxwin.h>**. The code in this function relies on the *EDITTEXT* resource directive (line 89) in the resource file to ensure, via the *ES_NUMBER* edit style, that the edit box only permits numeric input into the edit box. If the user presses a non-numeric key, a beep sounds. Non-numeric characters cannot be input or displayed when the **ES_NUMBER** edit style is set.

Lines 37 through 41

```
itoa( m_nTotal, szText, 10 );       // convert total to text

pTotal->SetWindowText( szText );    // display total
pNum->SetWindowText( "" );          // clear input
pNum->SetFocus();                   // next input to Number
```

convert the value in **m_nTotal** from **int** to a character string and store it in **szText** for *SetWindowText* to display in the edit box pointed to by **pTotal**. **SetWindowText** is inherited from **CWnd**. Lines 40 and 41 clear the edit box by setting its text to the null string (**""**), and give it the focus (i.e., make it the active control in the window) by calling *SetFocus* so that the user will not have to click the cursor in this field before entering the next number.

Message handler **OnClear** (line 45) handles the message when the user clicks the **Clear** button.

Lines 47 through 52

```
CEdit *pTotal = ( CEdit *)( GetDlgItem( IDC_TOTAL ) );
CEdit *pNum   = ( CEdit *)( GetDlgItem( IDC_NUMBER ) );

m_nTotal = 0;                       // clear the total
pTotal->SetWindowText( "" );        // clear the edit box
pNum->SetFocus();                   // next input to Number
```

get the addresses of the edit boxes by calling **GetDlgItem** and passing it the appropriate control ID, set **m_nTotal** to zero, display an empty string in the **Total:** edit box and set the focus to the **Enter a number:** edit box. This code is short because all the layout and other properties of the controls are defined in the resource file.

Lines 65 through 67

```
CAdditionDialog additionDialog;
additionDialog.DoModal();
return FALSE;
```

are a modification of the frame window application "boilerplate" code (e.g., lines 61 through 70 in Fig. 2.11) specifically for dialog-based applications. This code creates the **CAdditionDialog** object and makes it the main window of the application. MFC function **DoModal** is called to display the dialog as a *modal window* (i.e., no other windows in the program can be interacted with until this dialog is closed). A value of **FALSE** is returned to indicate that the application has ended.

Resource definition file **Addition.rc** (line 78) defines the **Addition** dialog window and the controls it contains. Lines 83 through 86

```
Addition DIALOG  50, 50, 130, 130
STYLE DS_MODALFRAME | WS_POPUP | WS_CAPTION | WS_SYSMENU

CAPTION "Addition Dialog Box"
```

define our **Addition** window to be a dialog window (i.e., *DIALOG*) located on the screen 50 pixels from the left, 50 pixels from the top and its size to be 130 *horizontal dialog units* wide and 130 *vertical dialog units* high. Horizontal dialog units are 1/4 the width of a character and vertical dialog units are 1/8 the height of a character.

Dialog units allow automatic adjustment of control sizes when the font size changes. [*Note:* To experiment with scaling dialog units, add the line *FONT 8, "MS Sans Serif"* immediately after the **CAPTION** line and compile and run the application, then change the 8 to 12 and compile and run it to see the dialog box and everything in it scale-up proportionally.]

The **STYLE** resource definition statement (line 84) creates the window's characteristics by combining multiple styles. Symbols for *Windows styles* have the prefix **WS_**, and symbols for *dialog styles* have the prefix **DS_**. Dialog-style *modal frame,* **DS_MODALFRAME**, indicates that other windows in the application cannot be accessed until the frame is closed. Windows-style *popup* **WS_POPUP** indicates a stand-alone window—not a child window that appears within another window. Windows-style *caption,* **WS_CAPTION**, indicates a title bar. Windows-style *sysmenu,* **WS_SYSMENU**, indicates a system menu containing **Move** and **Close** menu items (accessed by right-clicking the title bar) and a close button (i.e., the button containing an **x**) on the title bar. The title bar displays the text **Addition Dialog Box**.

Line 88

```
LTEXT            "Enter a number:", IDC_STATIC, 30, 20, 50, 8
```

defines a *static control,* a simple control that displays text and does not generate any messages. The text displayed is left-aligned. Other static controls are **CTEXT** and **RTEXT** for centered text and right-aligned text, respectively. Because a static control does not generate messages or need to be accessed by the program, it does not require a unique control identifier. **IDC_STATIC** is a common MFC identifier (predefined as -1), used for all static controls. The values *(30, 20)* are the top-left corner dialog unit coordinates and *(50, 8)* are the edit box width and height (in dialog units) that define the region text is displayed.

Line 89

```
EDITTEXT          IDC_NUMBER, 30, 30, 70, 16, ES_NUMBER
```

defines an edit box with the resource identifier **IDC_NUMBER** (defined on line 74). The resource identifier is used in message handler **OnAdd** at line 24 to get the address of the edit text object. The edit box appears at dialog window position *(30, 30)* dialog units. The width and height are 70 and 16 dialog units, respectively. The edit style (i.e., *ES_NUMBER*) specifies that only numeric input should be accepted. If the user presses a non-numeric key, a beep sounds and the character will not be accepted. The **EDITTEXT**'s *capacity* (i.e., the maximum number of characters that can be displayed) is equal to the **EDITTEXT**'s horizontal size (in dialog units) divided by 4, minus 1.

Line 91

```
DEFPUSHBUTTON     "Add", IDC_ADD, 50, 50, 30, 15
```

defines a default button **Add** with a caption "**Add**" and a message identifier **IDC_ADD**. The button appears at location *(50, 50)* and its size is 30 by 15 dialog units. The user can either click this button with the mouse or (because this is the default button) press the *Enter* key to send the **IDC_ADD** message.

The statements on lines 93 through 95

```
LTEXT             "Total:", IDC_STATIC, 30, 70, 20, 8
EDITTEXT          IDC_TOTAL, 30, 80, 70, 16,
                  ES_READONLY | NOT WS_TABSTOP
```

display the left-justified label **Total:** and the edit text control. Line 94 gives the edit text the identifier **IDC_TOTAL**, displays it at *(30, 80)* and sets its size to 70 by 16 dialog units. Line 95 sets its edit style to be read-only (**ES_READONLY**) and its window style (**NOT WS_TABSTOP**) not to receive focus when the user presses the *Tab* key to transfer the focus from one control to another. Removing output controls from the tab list makes it easier for the user to tab to input controls and buttons. Read-only edit boxes have a gray background, indicating that the edit box does not accept input.

The directive on lines 97 and 98

```
PUSHBUTTON        "Clear", IDC_CLEAR, 50, 100, 30, 15,
                  NOT WS_TABSTOP
```

creates a button labeled **Clear** with identifier **IDC_CLEAR** and displays it at coordinates *(50, 100)* with a size of 30 by 15 (dialog units). Style *WS_TABSTOP* is disabled to prevent the **Clear** button from receiving the focus when the user presses the *Tab* key to transfer the focus between controls.

Summary

- MFC is a class hierarchy a programmer can use to build Windows applications. MFC implements common characteristics of windows in base classes for other derived classes to use.

- A class has functions and data. When one class is derived from another, it inherits the functions and data of its base class.

- Classes **CDialog** and **CFrameWnd** encapsulate functionality for creating windows. Class **CWinApp** encapsulates the functionality for creating and executing a Windows application, replacing the customary C++ function **main**.

- When a GUI event occurs, the Windows operating system sends a message to the program. Programming the functions that respond to these messages is called event-driven programming.
- MFC simplifies event-driven programming by providing an application framework, code that encapsulates many of the details of Windows programming and provides an object-oriented interface to Windows.
- In MFC, each message is identified by a unique number called a message identifier. Functions that execute in response to messages are called message handlers. Message identifiers are "tied" to message handlers by the message map.
- Visual C++ provides a resource description language to specify each GUI control's location, size, message identifier, etc. These resource description language statements are stored in a resource file. Resource files are identified by their **.rc** file extension.
- The resource compiler reads the resource file and translates the resource definition language statements into object code (i.e., machine language code) which is then linked with the application.
- MFC programmers prefix variable names with letters indicating the variable's data type and scope. This naming convention is commonly referred to as Hungarian notation.
- The MFC run-time functions (preexisting MFC code that your program will call) are contained in a library (typically a library accessed at run time called a dynamic link library or DLL) that is separate from the standard C++ run-time library.
- The application framework header file **<afxwin.h>** defines classes (e.g., **CFrameWnd**, **CWinApp**, etc.) and includes other header files, such as **<afx.h>**, that are required to create an MFC application. Application framework headers begin with the prefix "**afx**".
- Constructors contain code for initializing an object of the class. A constructor always has the same name as the class, never returns a value and is executed when an object of the class is created (or instantiated).
- Use the arrow operator (**->**) to access member functions of an object through a pointer.
- A child window is a window that is always contained inside another window.
- Style **WS_VISIBLE** indicates that a window is visible.
- Style **WS_BORDER** indicates that a window has a border.
- Style **SS_CENTER** indicates that the text displayed in a **CStatic** window is centered.
- Destructors have the same name as their class prefixed with a tilde, **~**. Destructors cannot **return** values and cannot take arguments. Destructors are automatically called when an object is destroyed. A destructor for a class must explicitly **delete** any objects that were dynamically allocated with the **new** operator.
- "Boilerplate" code is a pattern of code that appears in multiple programs.
- Function **InitInstance** creates a window object and causes it to run. Function **InitInstance**'s return type is MFC type **BOOL** (an integer used by MFC for boolean true and false values.).
- Function **ShowWindow** displays a window. Its argument, **m_nCmdShow** is defined by the base class **CWinApp**. Variable **m_nCmdShow** is the main window's visibility option that is passed by Windows to the application to indicate whether the window is to be maximized when it is displayed.
- Function **UpdateWindow** forces the window to repaint itself.
- Windows applications are often written to display groups of related selections called menus. When the user clicks a menu name, that menu expands to display its list of menu items for the user to make a further selection by clicking a particular menu item.
- Function **MessageBox** displays a message box (i.e., a simple window containing a message).
- Prefix **afx_msg** is an MFC naming convention used to mark a message handler.

- String stream function **seekp** allows the programmer to control the position of the put pointer.
- Resource files contain resource definition language statements (i.e., a language that describes GUI elements such as menus, windows, controls, etc.). The resource definition language is not part of C++ programming language.
- MFC provides the class **CDialog** for creating windows called dialog boxes.
- Applications that only use dialog boxes for the GUI are called dialog-based applications.
- Function **GetDlgItem** gets an individual control's addresses.
- The **ES_NUMBER** edit style specifies that only numeric input is permitted.
- Function **SetFocus** transfers the focus.
- Function **SetWindowText** sets the text for any window, including windows, dialogs and edit boxes.
- Horizontal dialog units are 1/4 the width of a character and vertical dialog units are 1/8 the height of a character. Dialog units allow automatic control size adjustment when the font size changes.
- Symbols for Windows styles have the MFC prefix **WS_**, and symbols for dialog styles have the MFC prefix **DS_**.
- Edit-style **ES_READONLY** indicates that the edit text control is read only. Read-only edit boxes appear gray, indicating that the edit box does not accept input.
- Style **NOT WS_TABSTOP** prevents a control from receiving the focus when the user presses the *Tab* key to transfer the focus between controls.

Terminology

.rc file
Add to Project check box
afx.h
afx_msg
afxwin.h
application framework
arrow operator (**->**)
atoi function
base class
BEGIN_MESSAGE_MAP macro
"boilerplate" code
BOOL type
CAPTION resource
CButton class
CCmdTarget class
CDialog class
CEdit class
CFrameWnd class
child window
click the mouse
CListBox class
CMenu class
CObject class
console application
control
Create function in **CFrameWnd** class

Create function in **CStatic** class
CRect class
CStatic class
CWelcomeWindow class
CWinApp class
CWinThread class
CWnd class
DECLARE_MESSAGE_MAP() macro
#define preprocessor directive
delete operator
DEFPUSHBUTTON resource statement
default constructor
derived class
DIALOG resource statement
dialog-based application
dialog box
DoModal function in **CDialog** class
double-click the mouse
DS_MODALFRAME dialog style
EDITTEXT resource statement
END_MESSAGE_MAP macro
ends stream manipulator
ES_NUMBER edit style
ES_READONLY edit style
event
event-driven programming

event monitoring state
frame window
GetDlgItem function
GetWindowText function
graphical user interface (GUI)
GUI control
header file
hierarchy chart
horizontal dialog unit
Hungarian notation
IDC_STATIC control identifier
inherit
InitInstance function in **CWinApp** class
iomanip.h header file
LTEXT resource statement
m_nCmdShow data of **CWinApp** class
m_pMainWnd data of **CWinThread** class
member function
MENU resource statement
menu bar
menu item
MENUITEM resource statement
menus
message
message dispatcher
message handler
message identifier
message macro
message map
MessageBox class
MFC (Microsoft Foundation Classes)
MFC application
MFC classes
MFC control flow
MFC events
MFC objects
MFC programming
Microsoft Foundation Classes (MFC)
move the mouse
New dialog
new operator
New Project Information dialog
objects
ON_COMMAND macro
ON_COMMAND_RANGE macro

ostrstream class
output string stream
parent
POPUP resource statement
preprocessor directive
press a key
Project Settings dialog
PUSHBUTTON resource statement
put pointer
resource compiler
resource definition language
resource editor
resource file
scope of an identifier
screen coordinates
seekp function in **ostrstream** class
SendMessage function in **CWnd** class
SetFocus function in **CWnd** class
SetWindowText function in **CWnd** class
ShowWindow function in **CWnd** class
source file
SS_CENTER static control style
statement
static control
stdlib.h
strstrea.h
STYLE resource statement
system menu
Text File icon
type of an identifier
UpdateWindow function in **CWnd** class
Use MFC in a Shared DLL option
user friendly
vertical dialog units
Win32 Application project type
WM_CLOSE Windows message
WM_PAINT Windows message
WS_BORDER Windows style
WS_CAPTION Windows style
WS_CHILD Windows style
WS_OVERLAPPEDWINDOW Windows style
WS_POPUP Windows style
WS_SYSMENU Windows style
WS_TABSTOP Windows style
WS_VISIBLE Windows style

Common Programming Errors

2.1   Forgetting to use the **DECLARE_MESSAGE_MAP()** macro is a nonfatal logic error. Objects
       created from the class will not receive messages, so although your program may execute, it
       is likely to produce incorrect results.

2.2   Forgetting to add a message macro is a logic error. The expected message handler will not be called. Your program may execute but produce incorrect results.

2.3   Like any class library, MFC evolves over time. As a result, some MFC variables no longer have the same data type indicated by their Hungarian notation prefixes. This can lead to subtle programming errors.

2.4   Not setting the option **Use MFC in a Shared DLL** for a **Win32 Application** causes a linker error when building MFC applications.

2.5   Not including **<afxwin.h>** in an **MFC Win32 Application** program is a syntax error.

2.6   Resource definitions can use **#define** preprocessor symbols. Attempting to use keyword **const** is a syntax error.

Good Programming Practices

2.1   Using Hungarian notation promotes software readability by providing type and scope information about each variable's name.

2.2   Prefixing message handler names with **On** allows message handlers to be easily identified.

2.3   Beginning a message identifier with the prefix **IDM_** distinguishes it as an identifier for a menu.

2.4   Insert a blank line between adjacent groups of **ON_COMMAND** macros to show the boundaries between pop-up menus.

Look-and-Feel Observation

2.1   Most Windows applications provide a **File** menu as the left menu in the menu bar.

Software Engineering Observations

2.1   Messages can be generated by user actions, by other applications and by the operating system.

2.2   Predefined MFC message identifiers are located in header file **<afxwin.h>** and have values in the range 0 through 1023. Programmer-defined message identifiers have values in the range 1024 through 65535.

2.3   Resource files contain resource definition language statements, rather than C++ source code statements.

2.4   Hungarian notation is useful for distinguishing related variable names. For example, **CRocket** is a class and **pCRocket** is a pointer.

2.5   Hungarian notation is controversial—placing in a name a prefix that indicates the data type violates data abstraction and information hiding. Yet it can make a complex MFC C++ program easier to read.

2.6   To ensure data integrity, make your data **private** and make your member functions **public**.

2.7   MFC function prototypes use **BOOL** (defined as **int**) rather than ANSI/ISO C++ data type **bool**. **BOOL** cannot be changed to **bool** without causing fatal diagnostics.

2.8   Menus (versus dialogs) simplify GUIs by reducing the number of controls the user sees.

Self-Review Exercises

2.1   Fill in the blanks in each of the following:
   f) MFC stands for _____.
   g) A common naming convention used in MFC is _____.
   h) Resource files have a _____ file extension.
   i) Function _____ sets the text a window displays.

2.2   State whether each of the following is *true* or *false*. If *false*, explain why.
   a) MFC applications use message handler functions to respond to messages.
   b) In order to use MFC in a Win32 Application project, **Use MFC in a shared DLL** should must be selected.
   c) The header **<afxwin.h>** cannot be included in an MFC program.
   d) Resource definition language statements are compiled by the Visual C++ IDE.

2.3   Fill in the blanks in each of the following:
   a) The top-level class in the MFC hierarchy is _____.
   b) An MFC application is derived from MFC class _____.
   c) MFC class _____ encapsulates the functionality for a button.
   d) MFC class _____ encapsulates the functionality for creating customizable dialogs.

2.4   Fill in the blanks in each of the following:
   a) Function _____ creates a window object and causes it to run.
   b) Macro _____ associates the **WM_PAINT** message with the function **OnPaint**.
   c) The message map associates message _____ with message _____.

Answers to Self-Review Exercises

2.1   a) Microsoft Foundation Classes. b) Hungarian notation. c) **.rc**. d) **SetWindowText**.

2.2   a) True.
   b) True.
   c) False. header file **<afxwin.h>** is required by MFC applications.
   d) True.

2.3   a) **CObject**. b) **CWinApp**. c) **CButton**. d) **CDialog**.

2.4   a) **InitInstance**. b) **ON_WM_PAINT**. c) identifiers, handlers.

Exercises

2.5   Modify Fig. 2.8 to display a different, multiline message in a larger window.

2.6   Modify Fig. 2.12 to get three numbers from the user and display their sum, product, average, minimum value, maximum value and whether or not the three numbers input could be the sides of a right triangle. Use the Pythagorean theorem: $r^2 = a^2 + b^2$.

2.7   Modify Fig. 2.11 to include one more food option in each menu. Implement a menu option to let the manager increase all prices by a one-cent surcharge each time this option is selected.

2.8   Write a menu-driven program for buying a PC. Implement menus for CPU speed, memory size, monitor size, printer type and modem speed. Display the total cost of the system.

2.9   Write a menu-driven ice cream shop. Implement options for cone or dish, flavors, syrup (chocolate, strawberry and butterscotch) and toppings (sprinkles, whipped cream, nuts and cherry).

2.10   Write a program that plays the game of "guess the number" as follows: Your program chooses the number to be guessed by selecting an integer at random in the range 1 through 1000. The program creates a dialog box that displays:

```
I have a number between 1 and 1000.
Can you guess my number?
Please enter your first guess.
```

The player enters a first guess. The program displays a message box containing one of the following:

```
Excellent! You guessed the number!
Too low. Try again.
Too high. Try again.
```

If the player's guess is incorrect, your program should continue until the player finally gets the number correct. Your program should keep telling the player "**Too high**" or "**Too low**" to help the player "zero in" on the correct answer. Allow the user to play a new game without exiting the application.

2.11   Write a Tic-Tac-Toe referee program. The computer provides the display for two people to play on a 3-by-3 set of buttons. Use **SetWindowText("X")** to make a mark in the button the first player clicks and use **"O"** for the second player.

2.12   Modify the Tic-Tac-Toe program in Exercise 2.11 to play against the computer.

2.13   Write a calculator application that performs basic math operations such as addition, subtraction, multiplication and division.

2.14   Write an application that displays a message box when a button is clicked.

3

MFC Programming: Part II

Objectives

- To be able to write resource definition language statements for describing windows and controls.
- To use the password protection editw style.
- To be able to use message boxes and display predefined icons on them.
- To use string streams to format display text.
- To determine the mouse pointer location.
- To determine which mouse button was pressed.
- To determine which keyboard key was pressed.
- To be able to display text in a window.

Not a creature was stirring—not even a mouse; ...
Clement Clarke Moore
A Visit from St. Nicholas

Open sesame!
Anonymous (*A Thousand and One Nights*)

A client is to me a mere unit, a factor in a problem.
Sir Arthur Conan Doyle

In a time of drastic change it is the learners who inherit the future.
Eric Hoffer

I would rather make my name than inherit it.
William Makepeace Thackeray

The new electronic interdependence recreates the world in the image of a global village.
Marshall Herbert McLuhan

Outline

3.1 Introduction

In this chapter we introduce additional MFC capabilities. We show how to provide password protection for a dialog-based application containing edit text controls. We explain how to handle messages generated when the user clicks the mouse and how to determine the mouse pointer position. We discuss how to process messages generated by keyboard key presses, and we explain how to set the color and position of text displayed in a window.

3.2 Password Protection

When a user types information into an edit text control, each character typed is displayed in the control. This is the default behavior for this control and is appropriate for most applications. One disadvantage about displaying the text is that anyone can read what was input. You may not want certain confidential information such as social security numbers and passwords to be visible. Edit text controls can be made to display special characters (e.g., asterisks, *****) instead of the actual characters typed. These special characters hide or *mask* each character input. For example, if the user types "hello" and if the chosen special character is asterisk, the edit text control displays five asterisks.

Figure 3.1 displays a login dialog that prompts the user for a *user ID* (also called a *user name*) and a *password* (i.e., a "secret" word or phrase that confirms the user's identity). We use the *edit-style* **ES_PASSWORD**, a parameter in the resource file description of the edit text control, to instruct the control to mask characters input in the password field, thus providing *password protection* for the application. The user cannot access the application until a valid password is input in the edit text control. When a valid password is input, a message box is displayed showing the user ID. Clicking **OK** closes the message box and displays the application window allowing the user to proceed with the application. When an invalid password is input, a message box is displayed indicating that the user ID or password is invalid. For this example, any user ID can be input (in the screen captures we use **student5**). For this example, the only valid password is "**PassWord**".

Class **CLoginDialog** (line 4) consists of **private** members **m_szUserid** (a **char** array), **m_szPassword** (a **char** array) and **DECLARE_MESSAGE_MAP()** (a macro), and two **public** member functions—a constructor and a message handler.

The **CLoginDialog** constructor function (line 27) receives one pointer—a **char ***. The constructor invokes the base-class **CDialog** constructor. Pointer **lpszName** is passed to the base class. We will discuss the value passed into the **CLoginDialog** constructor shortly. In the body of the constructor (line 30) the first characters of **m_szUserid** and **m_szPassword** are set to null.

```
 1   // Fig. 3.1: CLogInDialog.h
 2   // login dialog
 3
 4   class CLoginDialog : public CDialog {
 5   public:
 6      CLoginDialog( char *lpszName );
 7      afx_msg void OnLogin();      // message handler for Log in
 8   private:
 9      char m_szUserid[ 17 ];
10      char m_szPassword[ 13 ];
11
12      DECLARE_MESSAGE_MAP()
13   };
14
15
16   class CMainWin : public CFrameWnd {
17   public:
18      CMainWin();
19      void login();
20   };
```

Fig. 3.1   Adding password protection to an edit text (part 1 of 7).

```
21   // Fig. 3.1: login.cpp
22   // login dialog
23   #include <afxwin.h>
24   #include "login_ids.h"
25   #include "CLoginDialog.h"
26
27   CLoginDialog::CLoginDialog( char *lpszName )
28      : CDialog( lpszName )
29   {
30      m_szUserid[ 0 ] = m_szPassword[ 0 ] = '\0';
31   }
32
33   // clicked the "Log in" button
34   afx_msg void CLoginDialog::OnLogin()
35   {
36      CEdit *pUserid;
37      CEdit *pPassword;
38
39      // get user ID value
40      pUserid = ( CEdit * ) GetDlgItem( IDC_USERID );
41      pUserid->GetWindowText( m_szUserid, 16 );
42
43      // get password value
44      pPassword = ( CEdit * ) GetDlgItem( IDC_PASSWORD );
45      pPassword->GetWindowText( m_szPassword, 12 );
46
47      // validate password
48      int j = strcmp( m_szPassword, "PassWord" );
49
```

Fig. 3.1   Adding password protection to an edit text (part 2 of 7).

```
50    if ( *m_szUserid != '\0' && j == 0 ) {
51       MessageBox( m_szUserid, "Access Granted",
52                   MB_ICONINFORMATION );
53       EndDialog( IDOK );            // Report login success
54    }
55    else {
56       MessageBox( "Invalid userid or password",
57                   "Login error",
58                   MB_ICONEXCLAMATION );
59
60       pPassword->SetWindowText( "" );  // clear password
61       pUserid->SetFocus();             // cursor in userid
62    }
63 }
64
65 BEGIN_MESSAGE_MAP( CLoginDialog, CDialog )
66    ON_COMMAND( IDC_LOGIN, OnLogin )    // Log in handler
67 END_MESSAGE_MAP()
68
69
70 // after validating user, main application continues
71 CMainWin::CMainWin()
72 {
73    Create( NULL, "Application Window",
74            WS_OVERLAPPEDWINDOW,
75            rectDefault );
76 }
77
78 // launch login dialog
79 void CMainWin::login()
80 {
81    CLoginDialog loginDialog( "Login" );
82
83    if ( loginDialog.DoModal() != IDOK )
84       SendMessage( WM_CLOSE );   // login failed
85 }
86
87
88 // application creates main window, requests login dialog
89 class CLoginApp : public CWinApp {
90 public:
91    BOOL InitInstance()
92    {
93       CMainWin *pMainWnd = new CMainWin;  // create window
94       m_pMainWnd = pMainWnd;              // set main window
95       pMainWnd->ShowWindow( m_nCmdShow ); // make visible
96       pMainWnd->UpdateWindow();           // force refresh
97
98       pMainWnd->login();                  // login dialog
99       return TRUE;                        // report success
100   }
101
102 } loginApp;
```

Fig. 3.1   Adding password protection to an edit text (part 3 of 7).

```
103  // Fig 3.1: login_ids.h
104  // define message numbers
105
106  #define IDC_USERID    2000
107  #define IDC_PASSWORD 2001
108  #define IDC_LOGIN     2002
```

Fig. 3.1   Adding password protection to an edit text (part 4 of 7).

```
109  // Fig03.01: login.rc
110  // login resources
111  #include <afxres.h>
112  #include "login_ids.h"
113
114  Login DIALOG  50, 50, 130, 130
115  CAPTION "User Authorization"
116  {
117      LTEXT          "Enter userid:",
118                     IDC_STATIC,   30,  20,  50,  8
119      EDITTEXT       IDC_USERID,   30,  30,  70, 16
120
121      LTEXT          "Password:",
122                     IDC_STATIC,   30,  50,  40,  8
123      EDITTEXT       IDC_PASSWORD, 30,  60,  70, 16,
124                     ES_PASSWORD
125
126      DEFPUSHBUTTON  "Log in", IDC_LOGIN, 50, 100, 30, 15
127  }
```

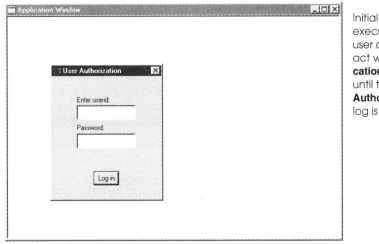

Initial GUI at execution. The user cannot interact with the **Application Window** until the **User Authorization** dialog is closed.

Fig. 3.1   Adding password protection to an edit text (part 5 of 7).

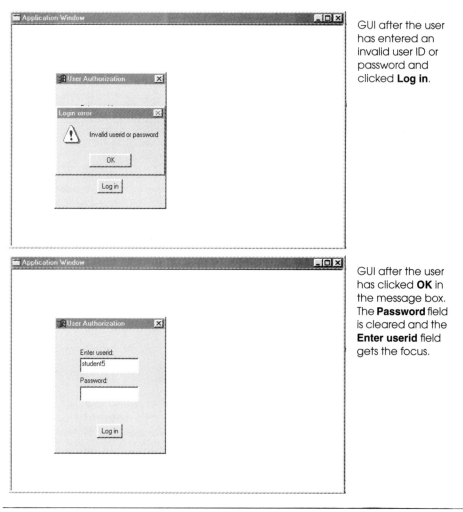

GUI after the user
has entered an
invalid user ID or
password and
clicked **Log in**.

GUI after the user
has clicked **OK** in
the message box.
The **Password** field
is cleared and the
Enter userid field
gets the focus.

Fig. 3.1   Adding password protection to an edit text (part 6 of 7).

Message handler **OnLogin** (line 34) is called when the user presses the **Log in**
button. Lines 36 and 37 declare two pointers—**pUserid** and **pPassword**—for pointing
to objects of type **CEdit**. MFC class **CEdit** is the class from which edit text controls are
created. We will use these pointers to retrieve the text input by the user into the edit text
controls. Line 40

```
pUserid = ( CEdit * ) GetDlgItem( IDC_USERID );
```

calls MFC function **GetDlgItem** to get a pointer to the edit text control identified by
IDC_USERID (defined on line 106). Because function **GetDlgItem** can return a pointer
to any control (e.g., edit texts, buttons, etc.) in the dialog box, the pointer returned by **Get-
DlgItem** is of type **CWnd *** (i.e., a base-class pointer for controls). The **CWnd *** returned
is cast to **CEdit *** and assigned to **pUserid**.

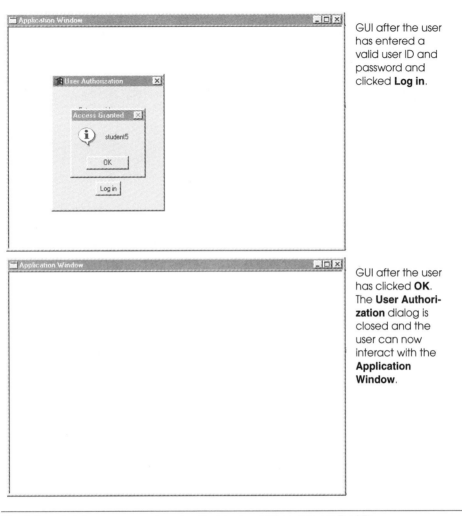

GUI after the user has entered a valid user ID and password and clicked **Log in**.

GUI after the user has clicked **OK**. The **User Authorization** dialog is closed and the user can now interact with the **Application Window**.

Fig. 3.1   Adding password protection to an edit text (part 7 of 7).

Now that we have a pointer to the edit text control, we can retrieve the edit text control's text. Line 41

```
pUserid->GetWindowText( m_szUserid, 16 );
```

calls function **GetWindowText** to get the text in the edit text control (**IDC_USERID**) pointed to by **pUserid** and store it in **m_szUserid**. The second argument, specifies the maximum number of characters that can be written to **m_szUserid**, including the null terminator character.

Lines 45

```
pPassword->GetWindowText( m_szPassword, 12 );
```

call function **GetWindowText** to get the text in the edit text control (**IDC_PASSWORD**) pointed to by **pPassword** and store it in **m_szPassword**. Although the text displayed in the edit text control is masked by asterisks, within the program the text assigned to **m_szPassword** is exactly as the user typed it.

For this example, our user ID and password verifications are straightforward. Line 48 calls function **strcmp** to test if the contents of **m_szPassword** are identical to the password **"PassWord"**. If they are identical, zero is assigned to **j**. For additional information on **strcmp**, see Section 5.12.2 of *C++ How to Program: Second Edition*.

The **if** condition (line 50)

```
*m_szUserid != '\0' && j == 0
```

determines if at least one character has been input for the user ID by testing the first character in **m_szUserid** against the null byte for inequality and determines if **j** (assigned the result of the string comparison on line 48) is equal to zero.

If the condition is true, a valid user ID and password have been input. Function **MessageBox** is called on line 51 to display a message box containing the user ID (e.g., **student5**), the title bar caption ("**Access Granted**") and a *message box information icon* (i.e., an *image* containing a blue "**i**" inside a white balloon—see Fig. 3.1). Constant **MB_ICONINFORMATION** instructs the message box to display the information icon.

After the user clicks **OK** to close the message box, MFC function **EndDialog** is called to close the **User Authorization** dialog with the MFC-defined **IDOK** value. The value passed to **EndDialog** is the return value for MFC function **DoModal** (line 83). We pass the MFC constant **IDOK** to **EndDialog** to indicate a successful login. We will say more about **IDOK** and **DoModal** momentarily.

If the **if** condition (line 50) evaluates to false because the user ID is missing or the password is incorrect, we display a message box (line 56) to inform the user that the login information is incorrect. We display the *message box exclamation icon* (i.e., an image containing a black "**!**" inside a yellow triangle—see Fig. 3.1). Constant **MB_ICONEXCLAMATION** represents the exclamation icon. A message box can display at most one icon from the icons listed in Fig. 3.2.

Constant	Icon	Description
MB_ICONSTOP		Displays stop icon. Typically used when a serious error or problem has occurred.
MB_ICONQUESTION		Displays question mark icon. Typically used to indicate that the user must make a decision.
MB_ICONEXCLAMATION		Displays exclamation point icon. Typically used to draw the user's attention to the message being displayed.
MB_ICONINFORMATION		Displays information icon. Typically used to give the user information about an action.

Fig. 3.2   MessageBox constants for icons.

When the user clicks the message box's **OK** button, the message box is closed. Because the user input is incorrect, we need to prepare the **User Authorization** dialog for the next login attempt by clearing the password edit text control and transferring the focus to the user ID edit text control. Lines 60 and 61

```
pPassword->SetWindowText( "" );   // clear password
pUserid->SetFocus();              // cursor in userid
```

clear the text displayed in the edit text control pointed to by **pPassword**—by passing a null string to **SetWindowText**, and transfer the focus to the edit text control pointed to by **pUserid**.

The message map (line 65) for **CLoginDialog** maps the message identifier **IDC_LOGIN** (line 108) to message handler **OnLogin** (line 34).

Line 16 derives class **CMainWin** from MFC class **CFrameWnd**. Class **CMainWin** represents the application the user wants to access. Class **CMainWin** contains two **public** member functions—a constructor and a function **login**. The constructor function (line 71) creates the window by calling function **Create**.

Function **login** (line 79) creates an instance of **CLoginDialog** with the line

```
CLoginDialog loginDialog( "Login" );
```

The argument passed to the **CLoginDialog** constructor is the **DIALOG** name (line 114) specified in the resource file. This string is passed to the **CDialog** base-class constructor (line 28). Base-class **CDialog** uses the resource description (lines 114 through 127) for the **Login DIALOG** to create our **CLoginDialog**. We will discuss the resource description language statements shortly.

The function call (line 83)

```
loginDialog.DoModal()
```

displays the **User Authorization** dialog by calling MFC function **DoModal**. Like message boxes, dialog boxes displayed by calling **DoModal** are modal, meaning other windows in the program cannot be accessed until the dialog is closed. Earlier, we mentioned that the value (e.g., **IDOK**) passed to **EndDialog** (line 53) is **DoModal**'s return value. When **IDOK** is passed to **EndDialog**, the dialog closes and the **if** condition on line 83

```
loginDialog.DoModal() != IDOK
```

is evaluated. Function **DoModal** returns *IDCANCEL* if the **User Authorization** dialog's close button is pressed. If the value returned by **DoModal** is not **IDOK**, we call class **CWnd** function **SendMessage** to send the window close message (**WM_CLOSE**) for **CMainWin**, which prevents unauthorized access by closing the application. Note that we do not explicitly write a message handler to close the window; we use the inherited message handler from **CFrameWnd** that provides the functionality for closing the window.

Lines 89 through 102 create an instance of our Win32 application. Line 98 calls function **login**, which creates and displays the **CLoginDialog** password dialog.

Programmer-defined header **"login_ids.h"** (line 103) defines the message identifiers used in **login.cpp** and in **login.rc**. On lines 106 and 107, the **IDC_USERID** and **IDC_PASSWORD** symbols are the identifiers for the dialog's **EDITTEXT** resources and line 108 defines the dialog's **DEFPUSHBUTTON** message identifier—**IDC_LOGIN**.

In the **login.rc** resource file (line 114)

```
Login DIALOG  50, 50, 130, 130
```

defines the **Login** dialog to be displayed at screen coordinates *(50, 50)* with a size of 130-by-130 dialog units. The dialog's caption is **"User Authorization"**.

The GUI components contained in the **Login** dialog are similar to those seen previously. A new feature is the **ES_PASSWORD** style, which is the *editing style* that displays asterisks to hide the characters typed in the **EDITTEXT**.

3.3 Processing Mouse Messages

Users interact with Windows programs typically with the keyboard and the mouse. The mouse is used to click buttons, move windows, resize windows, etc. Controls are capable of recognizing when the mouse is single-clicked, double-clicked, moved, dragged (moved with a button down) and when a button is released. The programmer writes *message handlers* to respond to these mouse messages and adds the appropriate *message macros* to the *message map*. In this section we introduce mouse message handling—an important Windows programming topic.

Figure 3.3 displays mouse coordinates on the screen and distinguishes left and right mouse-button clicks. The example demonstrates the basics of mouse message handling. As the user moves the mouse and clicks a mouse button, MFC sends messages to our message-handler functions. These functions call a function that displays the mouse coordinates at the mouse position and displays the status of the mouse buttons in the top-left corner of the screen. This program requires no new message definitions or resources, but a full-featured application would have buttons and menu definitions that require **.h** and **.rc** files.

The **CMouseWin** class definition (line 4) consists of one **private** member—macro **DECLARE_MESSAGE_MAP()**—and four **public** member functions—a constructor, a programmer-defined **showPoint** function and two message handlers. The constructor (line 23) creates the window by calling function **Create**.

```
1    // Fig 3.3: CMouseWin.h
2    // Mouse coordinates display
3
4    class CMouseWin : public CFrameWnd {
5    public:
6       CMouseWin();
7
8       // display mouse coordinates and mouse button status
9       void showPoint( UINT uFlags, CPoint point );
10
11      // mouse button handlers
12      afx_msg void OnLButtonDown( UINT uFlags, CPoint point );
13      afx_msg void OnRButtonDown( UINT uFlags, CPoint point );
14   private:
15      DECLARE_MESSAGE_MAP()
16   };
```

Fig. 3.3   Handling mouse messages (part 1 of 3).

```
17  // Fig 3.3: mouse.cpp
18  // Mouse coordinates display
19  #include <afxwin.h>
20  #include <strstrea.h>
21  #include "CMouseWin.h"
22
23  CMouseWin::CMouseWin()
24  {
25     Create( NULL, "Mouse Example", WS_OVERLAPPEDWINDOW );
26  }
27
28  // display mouse coordinates and mouse button status
29  void CMouseWin::showPoint( UINT uFlags, CPoint point )
30  {
31     CClientDC dc( this );        // get display context
32
33     static char sText[ 64 ];
34     static ostrstream s( sText, sizeof( sText ) );
35
36     s.seekp( 0 );     // reset to start of output string
37
38     // format data to display in sText buffer
39     s << "(" << point.x << ", " << point.y << ")";
40
41     // at point (x, y) on screen, display (x, y) value
42     dc.TextOut( point.x, point.y, sText, s.pcount() );
43
44     s.seekp( 0 );     // reset to start of output string
45     s << ( uFlags & MK_LBUTTON ? '*' : ' ' ) << " Left  "
46       << ( uFlags & MK_RBUTTON ? '*' : ' ' ) << " Right ";
47
48     // at 1,1 on screen, display mouse buttons' states
49     dc.TextOut( 1, 1, sText, s.pcount() );
50  }
51
52  // left mouse button handler
53  afx_msg void CMouseWin::OnLButtonDown( UINT uFlags,
54                                         CPoint point )
55  {
56     showPoint( uFlags, point );
57  }
58
59  // right mouse button handler
60  afx_msg void CMouseWin::OnRButtonDown( UINT uFlags,
61                                         CPoint point )
62  {
63     showPoint( uFlags, point );
64  }
65
66  BEGIN_MESSAGE_MAP( CMouseWin, CFrameWnd )
67     ON_WM_LBUTTONDOWN()    // left mouse button message handler
68     ON_WM_RBUTTONDOWN()    // right mouse button message handler
69  END_MESSAGE_MAP()
```

Fig. 3.3   Handling mouse messages (part 2 of 3).

```
70
71
72 // load main application window
73 class CMouseApp : public CWinApp {
74 public:
75    BOOL InitInstance()
76    {
77       m_pMainWnd = new CMouseWin;        // create window
78       m_pMainWnd->ShowWindow( m_nCmdShow );
79       m_pMainWnd->UpdateWindow();        // force refresh
80       return TRUE;                       // report success
81    }
82
83 } mouseApp;
```

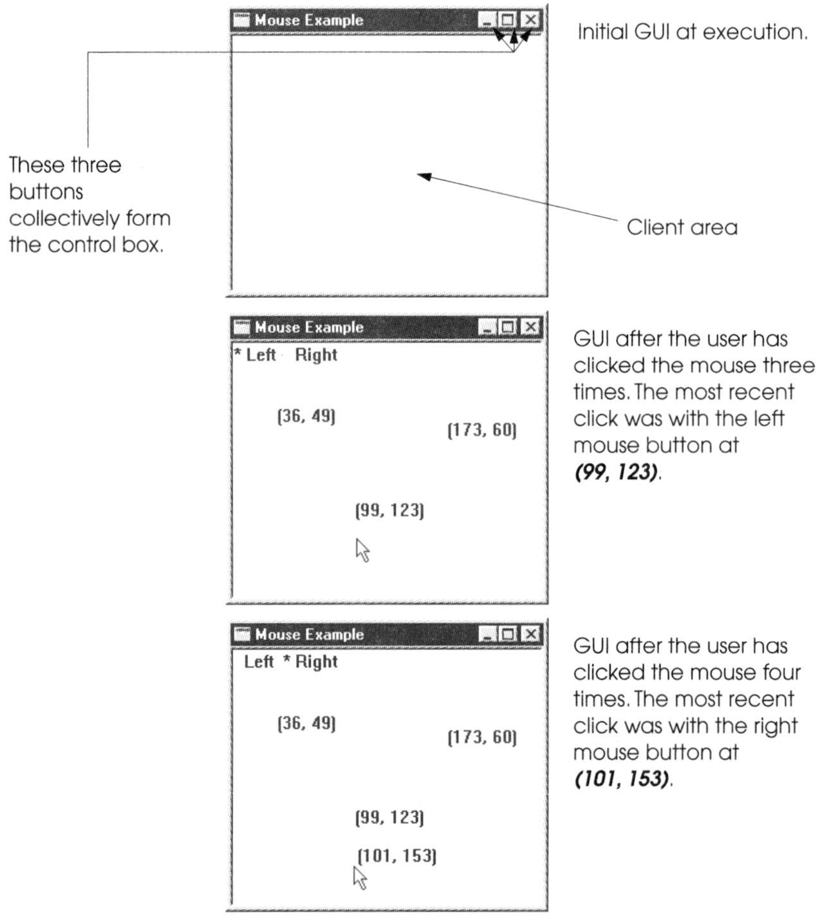
Mouse Example
Initial GUI at execution.
These three buttons collectively form the control box.
Client area
Mouse Example
* Left Right
(36, 49)
(173, 60)
(99, 123)
GUI after the user has clicked the mouse three times. The most recent click was with the left mouse button at (99, 123).
Mouse Example
Left * Right
(36, 49)
(173, 60)
(99, 123)
(101, 153)
GUI after the user has clicked the mouse four times. The most recent click was with the right mouse button at (101, 153).

Fig. 3.3 Handling mouse messages (part 3 of 3).

Function **showPoint** (line 29) determines the location of the mouse click, then draws draws text on the window indicating location of the mouse and the mouse button positions.

Function **showPoint** is called by message handlers *OnLButtonDown* (line 53—the message handler called when the left mouse button is clicked) and *OnRButtonDown* (line 60—the message handler called when the right mouse button is clicked). We *override* base-class message handlers **OnLButtonDown** and **OnRButtonDown**. See Section 9.6 in *C++ How to Program: Second Edition* for a discussion of overriding base-class members.

Function **showPoint** receives two arguments—the same two arguments **OnLButtonDown** and **OnRButtonDown** receive—one of type *UINT* (a Visual C++ **typedef** that represents an **unsigned int**—see Section 16.5 of *C++ How to Program: Second Edition* for a discussion of **typedef**) and another of type *CPoint* (an MFC class that represents one set of coordinates or a point). We use the **UINT** value to determine which mouse button was pressed and we use the **CPoint** object to get the coordinates of the mouse click. We will discuss how this is done momentarily.

Before we can draw on a window, we must get a special object—called a *device-context* object—that encapsulates the functionality for drawing on a window. More specifically we need a *CClientDC* device-context object because we want to draw inside the window's *client area* (i.e., the area inside the window border—see Fig. 3.3). Much of **CClientDC**'s functionality is derived from its base-class *CDC*. Line 31

```
CClientDC dc( this ); // get display context
```

gets the device context for **CMouseWin**'s (line 4) client area by passing the **this** pointer (see Section 7.5, in *C++ How to Program: Second Edition*) to the **CClientDC** constructor. Using the object **dc**, we can draw in the window's client area.

Lines 33 and 34 declare **static char** array **sText** (the text to draw on the client area) and construct **static ostrstream** object **s** (used to write **data** to the **char** array). Because we do not want our **ostrstream** object to be constructed—a time-consuming operation—every time function **showPoint** is invoked, we declare **s** to be **static**. Array **sText** must be **static** because **s** points to it.

Line 39

```
s << "(" << point.x << ", " << point.y << ")";
```

sends an open parenthesis, the *x*-coordinate, a comma followed by a space, the *y*-coordinate and a closing parenthesis to the **ostrstream s**. The *x*-coordinate and *y*-coordinate for the mouse click are stored in **CPoint** object **point** and are accessible through **public CPoint** data members **x** and **y**.

The contents of the **sText** are drawn on the client area with the statement (line 42)

```
dc.TextOut( point.x, point.y, sText, s.pcount() );
```

The **CDC** class function *TextOut* draws **sText**'s characters at the coordinate *(point.x, point.y)*. Function *pcount* returns the total number of characters written to **s** (i.e., the length of **sText**).

Because we want to write a new set of characters to **s**, we call **seekp** on line 44 to reset **s** to write to the beginning of **sText**.

The conditional expression in line 45

```
( uFlags & MK_LBUTTON ? '*' : ' ' )
```

determines if the left mouse button is pressed. The variable **uFlags** is combined with the MFC constant *MK_LBUTTON* using the bitwise AND operator (**&**) to determine if the bit corresponding to the left mouse button is set. If the bit is on, the conditional operator, (**?:**) evaluates to an asterisk. If the bit is off, the conditional operator evaluates to a space character. The right mouse button is tested in a similar manner using constant **MK_RBUTTON**. The bitwise AND operator and bit manipulation in general are discussed in detail in Section 16.7 of *C++ How to Program: Second Edition.*

Line 49

```
dc.TextOut( 1, 1, sText, s.pcount() );
```

calls **TextOut** to display the **sText**'s text at position *(1, 1)* in the window's client area.

Lines 66 through 69 define the message map for **CMouseWin**. Message macros **ON_WM_LBUTTONDOWN()** and **ON_WM_RBUTTONDOWN()** indicate that the message for a left-mouse click and the message for a right-mouse click will be handled. Lines 73 through 83 create an instance of our Win32 application.

3.4 Processing Keyboard Input Messages

Console applications use **cin** and **cout** for I/O operations and the previous example demonstrated some of the text output capabilities in MFC. We now explore the keyboard messages that allow us to monitor keystrokes. We use additional text output features and store all the text so we can repaint the screen when told to do so by MFC. We have to implement message handler *OnPaint* to update the screen with the stored data when the window receives a **WM_PAINT** message.

Figure 3.4 is a simple text editor program. When the user presses a key, the key's letter is drawn on the window.

```
1   // Fig. 3.4: CKeyboardWin.h
2   // keyboard input example
3
4   const int LINES = 24;          // maximum number of lines
5   const int LINE_LENGTH = 64;    // maximum characters per line
6   const int LINE_HEIGHT = 16;    // pixels between lines
7
8   // application window
9   class CKeyboardWin : public CFrameWnd {
10  public:
11     CKeyboardWin();
12
13     // refresh window when requested to by the system
14     afx_msg void OnPaint();
15
16     // process each character typed on keyboard
17     afx_msg void OnChar( UINT uChar, UINT uRepCnt, UINT uFlg );
18  private:
19     char m_asText[ LINES ][ LINE_LENGTH ]; // text to paint
20     int m_anLen[ LINES ];          // keep track of line lengths
21     int m_nLine;                   // line receiving keystrokes
22     DECLARE_MESSAGE_MAP()
23  };
```

Fig. 3.4   Handling keyboard messages (part 1 of 3).

```cpp
24   // Fig. 3.4: keyboard.cpp
25   // keyboard input example
26   #include <afxwin.h>
27   #include "CKeyboardWin.h"
28
29   // initialize main window
30   CKeyboardWin::CKeyboardWin()
31   {
32      m_nLine = 0;                  // empty text array
33      m_anLen[ m_nLine ] = 0;   // empty line of text
34
35      Create( NULL, "Keyboard Example", WS_OVERLAPPEDWINDOW,
36              CRect( 0, 0, 200, 200 ) );
37   }
38
39   // refresh window when requested to by the system
40   afx_msg void CKeyboardWin::OnPaint()
41   {
42      CPaintDC dc( this );      // get device context
43
44      int nPosition = m_anLen[ m_nLine ]++;
45
46      m_asText[ m_nLine ][ nPosition ] = '_';   // make a cursor
47
48      for ( int ln = 0; ln <= m_nLine; ln++ ) // paint lines
49         dc.TextOut( 1, LINE_HEIGHT * ln,
50                     m_asText[ ln ], m_anLen[ ln ] );
51
52      m_anLen[ m_nLine ]--;                        // remove cursor
53   }
54
55   // process each character typed on keyboard
56   afx_msg void CKeyboardWin::OnChar( UINT uChar, UINT uRepCnt,
57                                      UINT uFlg )
58   {
59      switch ( uChar ) {
60         case '\r':                            // start new line
61            m_nLine++;
62
63            if ( m_nLine >= LINES )
64               m_nLine = 0;                     // wrap around
65
66            m_anLen[ m_nLine ] = 0;
67            break;
68         case '\b':          // backspace erases previous char
69            if ( m_anLen[ m_nLine ] > 0 )
70               m_anLen[ m_nLine ]--;
71
72            break;
73         default:
74            int nPosition = m_anLen[ m_nLine ]++;
75
76            m_asText[ m_nLine ][ nPosition ] = uChar;
```

Fig. 3.4   Handling keyboard messages (part 2 of 3).

```
77
78               if ( m_anLen[ m_nLine ] >= LINE_LENGTH ) {
79
80                  if ( ++m_nLine >= LINES )
81                     m_nLine = 0;                      // wrap around
82
83                  m_anLen[ m_nLine ] = 0;
84               }
85        }
86
87        InvalidateRect( NULL );        // send WM_PAINT message
88 }
89
90 BEGIN_MESSAGE_MAP( CKeyboardWin, CFrameWnd )
91    ON_WM_CHAR()        // listen for any key press message
92    ON_WM_PAINT()       // listen for paint message
93 END_MESSAGE_MAP()
94
95 // application class creates window
96 class CKeyboardApp : public CWinApp {
97 public:
98    BOOL InitInstance()
99    {
100       m_pMainWnd = new CKeyboardWin;           // create window
101       m_pMainWnd->ShowWindow( m_nCmdShow );    // make it visible
102       m_pMainWnd->UpdateWindow();              // force refresh
103       return TRUE;                             // report success
104    }
105
106 } keyboardApp;
```

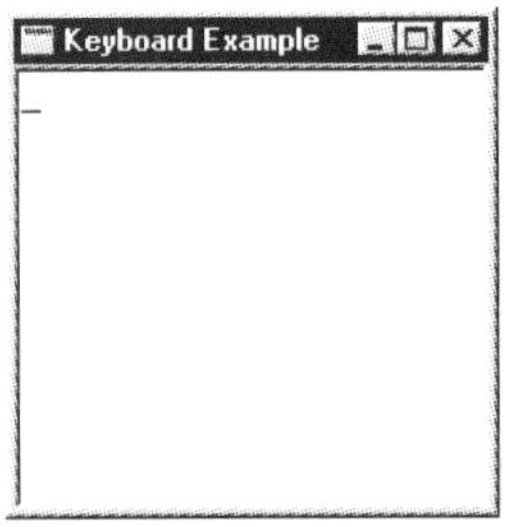

Initial GUI at execution. The underscore is the cursor.

GUI after the user has entered text. The cursor indicates where the next character typed will appear.

Fig. 3.4   Handling keyboard messages (part 3 of 3).

The **CKeyboardWin** class definition (line 9) consists of four **private** members—character array **m_asText**, integer array **m_anLen**, integer **m_nLine** and macro **DECLARE_MESSAGE_MAP()**—and three **public** member functions—a constructor and two message handlers.

The constructor (line 30) initializes **m_nLine** and **m_anLen[0]** to zero. Array **m_asText** stores the text to draw on the client area, and array **m_anLen** stores the length of each line of text in array **m_asText**. Variable **m_nLine** is the current row in **m_asText** where text is currently being written. Function **Create** is called on line 35 to create the window.

Message handler **OnPaint** (line 40) handles the *paint message* (i.e., the message passed by Windows when the client area must be redrawn). Paint messages are generated when a window is minimized, maximized, *exposed* (i.e., becomes visible when another window is moved), etc. Function **OnPaint** must use a *CPaintDC* device context to draw in the window. Much of **CPaintDC**'s functionality is derived from its base-class **CDC**.

Line 42

```
CPaintDC dc( this );    // get device context
```

creates a **CPaintDC** device-context object **dc** that is used to draw on **this** window's client area. Line 44

```
int nPosition = m_anLen[ m_nLine ]++;
```

makes room for the *cursor character* (i.e., a symbol indicating the position in the window where the next typed character will appear). The incremented line length is assigned to **nPosition**.

Line 46

```
m_asText[ m_nLine ][ nPosition ] = '_';    // make a cursor
```

writes an underscore character (the cursor) to the end of the current line in **m_asText**.

The **for** loop (line 48) calls **TextOut** to draw each line of text on the client area. Function **TextOut** is passed the top-left coordinates where drawing is to begin, the text to display and the number of characters of text to display. The top-left coordinates are *(1, LINE_HEIGHT * ln)*—we use a constant size for the text height. In Chapter 5, "MFC Graphics," we manipulate fonts and discuss how we can determine the actual font height. On line 52, we reset the line length to remove the cursor.

When the user types a character on the keyboard, Windows passes the *WM_CHAR* message to our program. The message dispatcher looks up the **WM_CHAR** message identifier and calls our overridden message handler **OnChar** (line 56).

Message handler **OnChar** receives three **UINT** arguments—*uChar*, *uRepCnt* and *uFlg*. Variable **uChar** is an integer that holds the character for the keyboard character pressed. Variables *uRepCnt* and *uFlg* provide lower-level capabilities such as counting the number of keystrokes that occur when the user holds down a key and the key's *transition state* (i.e., whether or not it is being pressed or released).

We use a **switch** statement (line 59) to process the key pressed. We provide special **case** handling for the *Enter* key, `'\r'`, and the *Backspace* key, `'\b'`. Figure 1.3 in *C++ How to Program: Second Edition* lists these escape sequences. All other characters are processed in the **default** case.

If *Enter* is pressed, the current line (i.e., **m_nLine**) is incremented by one (line 61). The **if** statement (line 63) resets the current line to zero (i.e., the first line of the client area) if the current line is greater than or equal to the maximum number of **LINES** (defined on line 4). Because we are at the beginning of a new line, line 66 sets the length of the line to zero.

If *Backspace* is pressed, the **if** condition on line 69 is tested. If the length of the current line is greater than zero, the length of the current line is reduced by one. Pressing *Backspace* does not physically remove the characters from the display. When a **WM_PAINT** message is handled, the entire contents of **m_asText** are displayed. We will discuss how the programmer can force this action by sending a **WM_PAINT** message momentarily.

All other characters are processed in the **default** case. Line 74 counts the characters per line as they are stored in **m_asText** (line 76). If the current text line has overflowed, (line 78), we advance to the next line of text. If the maximum number of lines has been exceeded, we reset to the first line of the text array.

MFC function *InvalidateRect* is called on line 87 to *repaint* (i.e., send a **WM_PAINT** message to the message dispatcher for our class) the client area. Argument **NULL** indicates that the entire client area should be repainted.

The message map (line 90) contains the message macros **ON_WM_CHAR()** and **ON_WM_PAINT()**, which indicate that we wish to handle **WM_CHAR** messages and **WM_PAINT** messages. Lines 96 through 106 create an instance of our Win32 application.

3.5 Text Output

MFC gives us complete control over the appearance of our text on the screen. The cost of this flexibility is that we have to manage the details. MFC offers all the objects, properties and functions we need. We must orchestrate these facilities to produce the display we want. Figure 3.5 demonstrates how to determine the size of the screen, control the color and placement of text on the screen, and determine the width and height (in pixels) of a string of text.

The **CTextWin** class definition (line 4) consists of one **private** member—macro **DECLARE_MESSAGE_MAP()**—and two **public** member functions—a constructor and a message handler. The constructor (line 28) calls function **Create** to create the window.

```
1   // Fig. 3.5: CTextWin.h
2   // Text display in the client area of a window
3
4   class CTextWin : public CFrameWnd {
5   public:
6      CTextWin();
7
8      // Refresh window when requested to by the system
9      afx_msg void OnPaint();
10  private:
11     DECLARE_MESSAGE_MAP()
12  };
```

Fig. 3.5   Drawing centered text in the client area of a window (part 1 of 3).

```
13   // Fig. 3.5: text.cpp
14   // Text display in the client area of a window
15   #include <afxwin.h>
16   #include "CTextWin.h"
17
18   char *aszText[] =
19   {
20      "Welcome to C++ and MFC!",
21      "This is text in the client area.",
22      " ",
23      "<---Neatly Centered--->",
24      NULL
25   };
26
27   // Create window for displaying text
28   CTextWin::CTextWin()
29   {
30      Create( NULL, "Text Example", WS_OVERLAPPEDWINDOW,
31              CRect( 100, 100, 400, 300 ) );
32   }
33
34   // Refresh window when requested to by the system
35   afx_msg void CTextWin::OnPaint()
36   {
37      CPaintDC dc( this );      // get paint display context
38
39      CRect rect;
40      GetClientRect( &rect ); // get size of client area
41
42      int nX = rect.right / 2;        // centered horizontally
43      int nY = rect.bottom / 4;       // 1/4 for top margin
44
45      // display lines of text centered in region of screen
46      for ( int nLine = 0; aszText[ nLine ] != NULL; nLine++ )
47      {
48         int nLength = strlen( aszText[ nLine ] );
49         CSize nCSizeText = dc.GetTextExtent( aszText[ nLine ],
50                                              nLength );
51
52         dc.SetTextColor( RGB( 255, 0, 0 ) );  // red text
53         dc.TextOut( nX - nCSizeText.cx / 2,   // center text
54                     nY,                       // vertical offset
55                     aszText[ nLine ],         // text to display
56                     nLength );                // char count
57
58         nY += nCSizeText.cy;  // advance to next line
59      }
60   }
61
62   BEGIN_MESSAGE_MAP( CTextWin, CFrameWnd )
63      ON_WM_PAINT()        // OnPaint handles WM_PAINT message
64   END_MESSAGE_MAP()
65
```

Fig. 3.6   Drawing centered text in the client area of a window (part 2 of 3).

```
66
67   // application creates main window
68   class CTextApp : public CWinApp {
69   public:
70      BOOL InitInstance()
71      {
72         m_pMainWnd = new CTextWin;           // create window
73         m_pMainWnd->ShowWindow( m_nCmdShow ); // make it visible
74         m_pMainWnd->UpdateWindow();          // force refresh
75         return TRUE;                          // report success
76      }
77
78   } textApp;
```

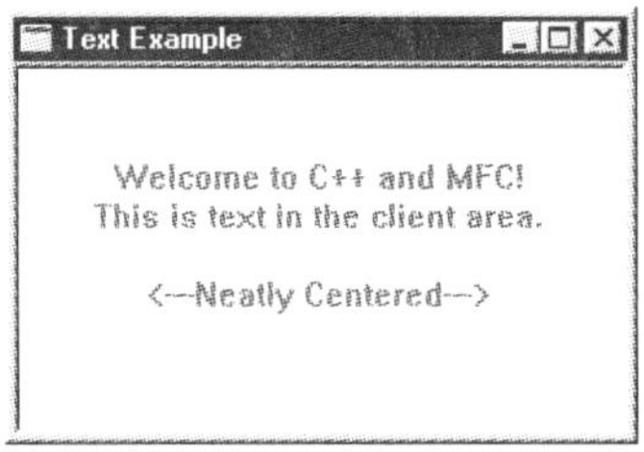

Fig. 3.7 Drawing centered text in the client area of a window (part 3 of 3).

Message handler **OnPaint** (line 35) handles the paint message. Line 37

```
CPaintDC dc( this );   // get paint display context
```

gets the device context for the **textApp**'s (line 78) client area by passing **this** to the **CPaintDC** constructor. In order to center the text drawn on the client area, we must get the width and height of the client area. Lines 39 and 40

```
CRect rect;
GetClientRect( &rect );   // get size of client area
```

create **CRect** object **rect** and pass its address to MFC function *GetClientRect*. Function **GetClientRect** populates **rect** with the top-left coordinates of the client area and the bottom-right coordinates of the client area.

To find the horizontal center of the text in the window (line 42), we divide the maximum *x* pixel location (i.e., the *x* value for the bottom-right coordinate stored in **public** member *right*) by two.

To leave one quarter of the window for the top margin (line 43), we divide the maximum *y* pixel location (i.e., the *y* value for the bottom-right coordinate stored in **public** member *bottom*) by four.

The **for** loop (lines 46) draws each string in **aszText** (line 18). Line 48 assigns the number of characters in **aszText[nLine]** to **nLength**.

MFC provides the **CDC** function *GetTextExtent* for determining a string's width and height. Function **GetTextExtent** returns a *CSize* object that contains **public** data members *cx*, which contains the width, and *cy*, which contains the height. Line 49 passes a string from **aszText** and the string's length to **GetTextExtent**.

Colors are created by combining three integer values (each of which is in the range 0 to 255, inclusive) that represent the amount of red, green and blue, respectively. Windows macro **RGB** combines these three integer values to create a color value. On line 52, the expression

```
RGB( 255, 0, 0 )
```

evaluates to the color red. The first number, **255**, provided to the macro specifies the maximum intensity of red. The second and third arguments (both **0**) specify that green and blue, respectively have zero intensity. Function **SetTextColor** sets the drawing color for the text to red. Any text written to the client area from this point onward will be red. We discuss color in more depth in Chapter 5, "MFC Graphics."

Line 53

```
dc.TextOut( nX - nCSizeText.cx / 2,    // center text
            nY,                         // vertical offset
            aszText[ nLine ],           // text to display
            nLength );                  // char count
```

calls function **TextOut** to display the text contained in **aszText**. The first argument centers the text horizontally in the client area. The horizontal center is calculated by dividing the width of the string (**nCSizeText.cx**) by 2 and subtracting the result from the horizontal center (**nX**) of the client area. The second argument (**nY**) is the y-coordinate for the display. The third argument specifies the text to display, and the last argument specifies the number of characters to display.

Line 58

```
nY += nCSizeText.cy;   // advance to next line
```

adds the string height to **nY**, which prevents the lines of text from overlapping.

Run this program and resize the window. The text position will remain centered left to right and keep a quarter-window top margin. Notice what happens when you shrink the window to be smaller than the text. The text is neatly *clipped*—nothing is displayed outside the client area.

The message map (lines 62) contains the message macro **ON_WM_PAINT()** indicating that we wish to handle **WM_PAINT** messages. Lines 68 through 78 create an instance of our Win32 application.

Summary

- Constant **MB_ICONINFORMATION** instructs a message box to display the information icon.
- MFC function **EndDialog** closes a dialog box. The value passed to **EndDialog** is the return value for **CDialog** function **DoModal**.
- Constant **MB_ICONEXCLAMATION** instructs a message box to display the exclamation icon.
- Constant **MB_ICONQUESTION** instructs a message box to display the question mark icon.
- Constant **MB_ICONSTOP** instructs a message box to display the stop icon.
- Like message boxes, a dialog box displayed by calling **DoModal** block access to other windows in the application until it is closed.
- Style **ES_PASSWORD** is the editing style that displays asterisks to mask characters typed in an edit box control.

- The mouse is used to click buttons, move windows, resize windows, etc. Controls are capable of recognizing when the mouse is single-clicked, double-clicked, etc.
- Message handler **OnLButtonDown** handles a left mouse button click.
- Message handler **OnRButtonDown** handles a right mouse button click.
- MFC class **CPoint** represents one pair of coordinates or a point. Class **CPoint** contains **public** data members **x** and **y**.
- A device context is an object that encapsulates the functionality for drawing on a window.
- A **CClientDC** device context encapsulates the functionality to draw on a window's client area (i.e., the area inside the window border).
- A **CPaintDC** device context encapsulates the functionality to draw in a window. This device context is used in message handler **OnPaint**.
- MFC function **TextOut** draws characters onto a device context.
- Function **pcount** returns the total number of characters written to an **ostrstream**.
- Variable **uFlags** can be combined with MFC constant **MK_LBUTTON** using the bitwise AND operator **&** to determine if the bit corresponding to the left mouse button is set.
- Variable **uFlags** can be combined with MFC constant **MK_RBUTTON** using the bitwise AND operator **&** to determine if the bit corresponding to the right mouse button is set.
- Message map macros **ON_WM_LBUTTON()** and **ON_WM_RBUTTON()** indicate that the message for a left mouse click and the message for a right mouse click will be handled.
- Paint messages are generated when a window is minimized, maximized, exposed (i.e., becomes visible when another window that was covering or partially covering the window is moved), etc.
- When the user types a character on the keyboard, Windows passes the **WM_CHAR** message into the program. The message dispatcher looks up the **WM_CHAR** message identifier and calls message handler **OnChar**.
- Message handler **OnChar** receives three **UINT** arguments—**uChar**, **uRepCnt** and **uFlg**. Variable **uChar** is an integer that stores the character for the keyboard key pressed. Variables **uRepCnt** and **uFlg** provide lower-level capabilities such as counting the number of keystrokes that occur when the user holds down a key and the key's transition state (i.e., whether or not it is being pressed or released).
- MFC function **InvalidateRect** is called to repaint (i.e., send a **WM_PAINT** message to the message dispatcher for our class) the client area. Argument **NULL** indicates that the entire client area should be repainted.
- Function **GetClientRect** populates a **CRect** object with the top-left coordinate of the client area as *(0,0)* and the bottom-right coordinate of the client area as its size.
- MFC provides function **GetTextExtent** for determining a string's width and height. Function **GetTextExtent** returns a **CSize** object that contains **public** data members **cx**—which contains the width and **cy** —which contains the height.
- Colors are created by combining three integer values (each of which is in the range 0 to 255, inclusive). MFC macro **RGB** combines the red, green and blue integer values to create a color value.
- MFC function **SetTextColor** sets the drawing color for the text drawn on a device context.

Terminology

bottom data member of **CRect**	client area
CClientDC class	clipped
click the mouse	clipping

control box

CPoint class

CRect class

cursor character

device context

DoModal function

double click the mouse

drag the mouse

edit text control

ES_PASSWORD edit style

exclamation point icon

expose a window

GetClientRect function of class **CWnd**

GetTextExtent function of class **CDC**

GetWindowText function of class **CWnd**

IDCANCEL constant

IDOK constant

information icon

InvalidateRect function of class **CWnd**

left data member of **CRect**

left mouse button

maximize a window

message box exclamation icon

message handler

message macro

message map

minimize a window

MB_ICONEXCLAMATION constant

MB_ICONINFORMATION constant

MB_ICONQUESTION constant

MB_ICONSTOP constant

MK_LBUTTON constant

MK_RBUTTON constant

mouse

mouse button

mouse message handling

mouse pointer position

move the mouse

ON_WM_PAINT macro

OnChar message handler

OnLButtonDown message handler

OnPaint message handler

OnRButtonDown message handler

overriding base-class members

password

password protection

question mark icon

.rc file

RGB color

RGB macro

right data member of **CRect**

right mouse button

SetTextColor function of class **CDC**

ShowWindow function of class **CWnd**

single-click the mouse

stop icon

string stream

TextOut function of class **CDC**

top data member of **CRect**

uFlags variable

UINT data type

WM_CHAR message

WM_PAINT message

Self-Review Exercises

3.1   State whether each of the following is *true* or *false*. If *false*, explain why.

    a) A device context is MFC's connection to a CD-ROM player.

    b) Password protection requires the user to type asterisks to mask their input.

    c) Message handler **OnRButtonDown** handles a right mouse button click.

    d) Function **TextOut** draws text on a device context.

3.2   Fill in the blanks in each of the following:

    a) MFC message box icon _____ instructs a message box to display an exclamation icon.

    b) Function _____ returns the number of characters written to an **ostrstream**.

    c) Class **CRect** has **public** data member _____ and **public** data member _____.

    d) MFC message box icon _____ instructs a message box to display a stop icon.

Answers to Self-Review Exercises

3.1   a) False. A device context encapsulates the functionality for drawing on a window.

    b) False. Password protection is the resource definition editing-style **ES_PASSWORD**.

c) True.

d) True.

3.2   a) **MB_ICONEXCLAMATION**. b) **pcount**. c) **x, y**. d) **MB_ICONSTOP**.

Exercises

3.3   Modify Fig. 2.11 to add password protection for employees and managers.

3.4   Modify Fig. 2.11 to display the customer's order as items are selected.

3.5   Modify Exercise 3.4 to delete items from the order by right-clicking an item.

3.6   Modify Exercise 3.5 to report total sales, sales per item, sales per employee and current prices per item.

3.7   Modify Fig. 3.3 to make a simple drawing program. Draw an asterisk where the user clicks on the screen. Keep an array of coordinates for redrawing the screen.

3.8   Modify the keyboard example for Fig. 3.4 to delete lines by right-clicking them and to insert a blank line by left-clicking a line. Allow the keyboard arrow keys to be used to move the cursor.

4

MFC Graphical User Interface Controls

Objectives

- To be able to create multiline edit text controls.
- To be able to create a group box.
- To be able to create and use check box controls.
- To be able to create and use radio button controls.
- To be able to create and use list box controls.
- To be able to create and use combo box controls.

You can't depend on your judgment when your imagination is out of focus.
Mark Twain

I shall be telling this with a sigh
Somewhere ages and ages hence:
Two roads diverged in a wood, and I—
I took the one less travelled by,
And that has made all the difference.
Robert Frost

In automobile terms, the child supplies the power but the parents have to do the steering.
Dr. Benjamin Spock

Our ideals, laws, and customs should be based on the proposition that each generation in turn becomes the custodian rather than the absolute owner of our resources—and each generation has the obligation to pass this inheritance on to the future.
Alden Whitman

You pays your money and you takes your choice.
John Banister Tabb

Outline

4.1 Introduction

Graphical user interfaces (GUIs) are created using controls. In Chapters 2 and 3, we introduced the edit text control and the button control. In this chapter, we introduce controls that will substantially upgrade your GUIs. Once you learn a "critical mass" of MFC control classes, you can easily learn more by browsing the online documentation. When you complete this chapter, you will be able to build more substantial Windows applications using MFC and have a better understanding of Windows GUIs.

4.2 Multiline Edit Text Controls

An edit text control (also called an *edit box*) is a rectangular area where text can be input or displayed. The edit text controls presented so far have been *single-line controls* (i.e., they display exactly one line of text). In this section, we introduce how to create and manipulate *multiline edit text controls*—edit text controls that display more than one line of text.

Figure 4.1 allows the user to enter text in a multiline edit text control. When the user clicks **Count**, the program counts the number of characters entered and displays the count in the same edit text control. This demonstrates input and output to the same edit text control. In the exercises, we ask you to use separate edit text controls for input and output.

```
1   // Fig. 4.1: CEditTextDialog.h
2   // multiline edit text example
3
4   const int MAX_TEXT = 128;
5
6   class CEditTextDialog : public CDialog {
7   public:
8      CEditTextDialog( char *lpszName );
9      afx_msg void OnCount();      // clicked the "Count" button
10
11  private:
12     char m_szText[ MAX_TEXT + 1 ];
13
14     DECLARE_MESSAGE_MAP()
15  };
```

Fig. 4.1   Creating and using a multiline edit text control (part 1 of 5).

```
16  // Fig. 4.1: edittext.cpp
17  // multiline edit text example
18  #include <afxwin.h>
19  #include <strstrea.h>
20  #include "edittext_ids.h"
21  #include "CEditTextDialog.h"
22
23  // Dialog constructor
24  CEditTextDialog::CEditTextDialog( char *lpszName )
25     : CDialog( lpszName )    // base class constructor
26  {
27     m_szText[ 0 ] = '\0';
28  }
29
30  // count the characters in the edit text control
31  afx_msg void CEditTextDialog::OnCount()
32  {
33     // get address of edit control
34     CEdit *pText = ( CEdit * ) GetDlgItem( IDC_TEXT );
35     pText->GetWindowText( m_szText, MAX_TEXT );
36
37     // display length of text read from edit text control
38     static char szBuf[ 20 ];
39     static ostrstream str( szBuf, 20 );
40
41     str.seekp( 0 );
42     str << "Text length = " << strlen( m_szText ) << ends;
43     pText->SetWindowText( szBuf );
44  }
45
46  BEGIN_MESSAGE_MAP( CEditTextDialog, CDialog )
47     ON_COMMAND( IDC_COUNT, OnCount )
48  END_MESSAGE_MAP()
49
50  // start dialog-based application
51  class CEditApp : public CWinApp {
52  public:
53     BOOL InitInstance()
54     {
55        CEditTextDialog editTextDialog( "EditText" );
56        editTextDialog.DoModal();    // run dialog
57        return FALSE;                // finished
58     }
59
60  } editApp;
```

Fig. 4.1   Creating and using a multiline edit text control (part 2 of 5).

The **CEditTextDialog** class definition (line 6) consists of two **private** members—array **m_szText** and macro **DECLARE_MESSAGE_MAP()**—and two **public** member functions—a constructor and a message handler. The constructor (line 24) initializes the dialog and sets the first character of **m_szText** to the null byte (line 27).

```
61   // Fig 4.1:  edittext_ids.h
62   // define edit text message identifiers
63
64   #define IDC_TEXT      2001
65   #define IDC_COUNT     2002
```

Fig. 4.1   Creating and using a multiline edit text control (part 3 of 5).

```
66   // Fig 4.1: edittext.rc
67   // multiline edit text resource file
68   #include <afxres.h>
69   #include "edittext_ids.h"
70
71   EditText DIALOG  50, 50, 130, 130
72   CAPTION "Edit"
73   {
74      LTEXT            "Enter text:",
75                       IDC_STATIC, 30,  20, 50, 8
76
77      // Define edit text with identifier IDC_TEXT,
78      // position (30, 30) and size 70 by 64
79      // edit styles multiline and auto vertical scroll
80      EDITTEXT         IDC_TEXT,   30,  30, 70, 64,
81                       ES_MULTILINE | ES_WANTRETURN | WS_VSCROLL
82
83      DEFPUSHBUTTON    "Count",
84                       IDC_COUNT,  50, 100, 30, 15
85   }
```

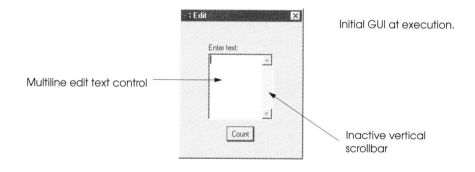

Initial GUI at execution.

Multiline edit text control

Inactive vertical scrollbar

Fig. 4.1   Creating and using a multiline edit text control (part 4 of 5).

Message handler **OnCount** (line 31) is called when the **Count** button is clicked. On line 35, the edit text control's text is retrieved and stored in **m_szText**. Lines 38 and 39 declare a character array—**szBuf** for storing text—and create an **ostrstream** object—**str** for writing to **szBuf**. Line 42 writes the length of the text input to **szBuf** via **str**, and line 43 displays the contents of **szBuf** in the edit text control by calling **SetWindowText**.

Lines 46 through 48 define the message map for **CEditTextDialog**. Message identifier **IDC_COUNT** (defined on line 65) is mapped to message handler **OnCount**. Lines 51 through 60 create an instance of our Win32 application.

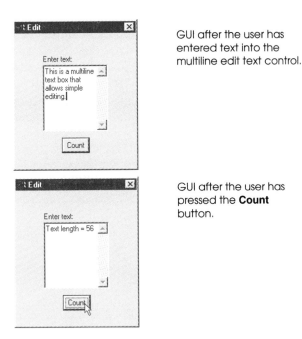

GUI after the user has
entered text into the
multiline edit text control.

GUI after the user has
pressed the **Count**
button.

Fig. 4.1   Creating and using a multiline edit text control (part 5 of 5).

The resource file (line 66) contains our **DIALOG** description for **EditText**. Line 80

```
EDITTEXT    IDC_TEXT, 30, 30, 70, 64,
            ES_MULTILINE | ES_WANTRETURN | WS_VSCROLL
```

defines an **EDITTEXT** at coordinates *(30, 30)* with size 70-by-64 dialog units. *Horizontal dialog units* are 1/4 the typical character width of the current font. *Vertical dialog units* are 1/8 the typical character height. Style ***ES_MULTILINE*** specifies that the edit text is multiline. By default, edit text controls do nothing when the *Enter* key (also called the *Return* key) is pressed. This behavior allows other controls (such as **DEFPUSHBUTTON**s) to respond when the *Enter* key is pressed. Style ***ES_WANTRETURN*** allows an edit text control to respond by displaying a carriage-return line-feed combination when the *Enter* key is pressed. This behavior allows the edit text control to behave much like a text editor—when *Enter* is pressed the cursor is positioned at the beginning of the next line. Style ***WS_VSCROLL*** specifies that the edit text control should display a *vertical scrollbar*. By default the scrollbar is disabled (i.e., grayed), the scrollbar is enabled when the number of lines input by the user exceeds the number of lines the edit text can display.

Software Engineering Observation 4.1

Dialog units make it easy to scale GUI controls to text. If you want a control that is 8 characters wide and 2 characters high, a 32-by-16 dialog unit box will do.

4.3 Check Boxes

Check boxes are controls that present the user with boolean choices (i.e., true or false, yes or no, on or off). Whenever the user clicks a check box it toggles to the opposite state. If checked, the choice is selected (i.e., true) and if unchecked the choice is not selected (i.e., false). Check boxes are used to express options that have only one of two states—true or false. The state of one check box does not affect any other check box's state. The **AU-TOCHECKBOX** statement in the resource file is used to create a check box.

Look-and-Feel Observation 4.1

Check boxes present the user with choices from a group of items. At any time, multiple check boxes can be selected.

In Fig. 4.2, we create an MFC program that allows the user to select ice cream flavors via check boxes. The check boxes are placed in a *container* called a *group box* (i.e., the border titled **Flavors** in Fig. 4.2). Group boxes (also called *frames*) are *static controls*, because they do not generate any messages or respond to user actions. Group boxes visually indicate a group of related controls.

```
1   // Fig. 4.2: CCheckBoxDialog.h
2   // check box example
3
4   class CCheckBoxDialog : public CDialog {
5   public:
6      CCheckBoxDialog( char *lpszName );
7
8      afx_msg void OnOK();      // clicked the "OK" button
9
10  private:
11     // helper function combines two MFC calls in one
12     int GetButtonStatus( int nId );
13
14     DECLARE_MESSAGE_MAP()
15  };
```

Fig. 4.2   Creating and using check boxes (part 1 of 6).

```
16  // Fig. 4.2: checkbox.cpp
17  // check box example
18  #include <afxwin.h>
19  #include <strstrea.h>
20  #include "checkbox_ids.h"
21  #include "CCheckBoxDialog.h"
22
23  CCheckBoxDialog::CCheckBoxDialog( char *lpszName )
24      : CDialog( lpszName ) {}
25
26  // helper function combines two MFC calls in one
27  int CCheckBoxDialog::GetButtonStatus( int nId )
28  {
29     CButton *pCButton = ( CButton * ) GetDlgItem( nId );
30     return pCButton->GetCheck();
31  }
32
```

Fig. 4.2   Creating and using check boxes (part 2 of 6).

Look-and-Feel Observation 4.2

Use a group box to enclose a number of related check boxes. Logical groupings make a dialog box easier for the user to understand.

```
33   // overriding OnOK function
34   afx_msg void CCheckBoxDialog::OnOK() // clicked "OK" button
35   {
36      static char sMessage[ 64 ];
37      static ostrstream str( sMessage, 64 );
38      str.seekp( 0 );
39
40      int nChocolate  = GetButtonStatus( IDC_CHOCOLATE );
41      int nVanilla    = GetButtonStatus( IDC_VANILLA );
42      int nStrawberry = GetButtonStatus( IDC_STRAWBERRY );
43
44      str << "Flavor(s) Selected:\n\n";
45
46      if ( nChocolate )
47         str << "   Chocolate\n";
48
49      if ( nVanilla )
50         str << "   Vanilla\n";
51
52      if ( nStrawberry )
53         str << "   Strawberry\n";
54
55      if ( nChocolate + nVanilla + nStrawberry == 0 )
56         str << "   None\n";
57
58      str << ends;
59
60      MessageBox( sMessage, "Ice Cream" );
61   }
62
63   BEGIN_MESSAGE_MAP( CCheckBoxDialog, CDialog )
64      ON_COMMAND( IDOK, OnOK )
65   END_MESSAGE_MAP()
66
67
68   // start application, create dialog window
69   class CCheckBoxApp : public CWinApp {
70   public:
71      BOOL InitInstance()
72      {
73         CCheckBoxDialog checkBoxDialog( "CCheckBox" );
74         checkBoxDialog.DoModal();          // run dialog window
75         return FALSE;                      // exit
76      }
77
78   } checkBoxApp;
```

Fig. 4.2   Creating and using check boxes (part 3 of 6).

```
79  // Fig. 4.2: checkbox_ids.h
80  // check box message identifiers
81
82  #define IDC_CHOCOLATE  2200
83  #define IDC_VANILLA    2201
84  #define IDC_STRAWBERRY 2202
```

Fig. 4.2   Creating and using check boxes (part 4 of 6).

```
85   // Fig. 4.2: checkbox.rc
86   // check box resource file
87   #include <afxres.h>
88   #include "checkbox_ids.h"
89
90   CCheckBox DIALOG  50, 50, 110, 80
91   CAPTION "CheckBox"
92   {
93      GROUPBOX      "Flavors",    IDC_STATIC,      15,  5, 80, 50
94
95      AUTOCHECKBOX "Chocolate",  IDC_CHOCOLATE,   20, 15, 60, 10
96      AUTOCHECKBOX "Vanilla",    IDC_VANILLA,     20, 25, 60, 10
97      AUTOCHECKBOX "Strawberry", IDC_STRAWBERRY,  20, 35, 60, 10
98
99      DEFPUSHBUTTON "OK",        IDOK,            40, 60, 30, 15
100  }
```

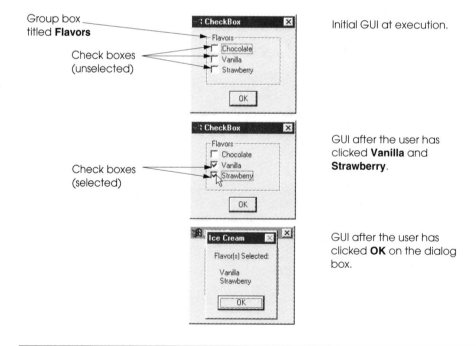

Fig. 4.2   Creating and using check boxes (part 5 of 6).

GUI after the user has clicked **OK** to close the message box.

Fig. 4.2   Creating and using check boxes (part 6 of 6).

The **CCheckBoxDialog** class definition (line 4) consists of two **private** members—programmer-defined function **GetButtonStatus** and MFC-defined macro **DECLARE_MESSAGE_MAP()**—and two **public** member functions—a constructor and a message handler. The constructor (line 23) invokes the base-class constructor.

Message handler **OnOk** (line 34) handles the message sent when **OK** is clicked by the user. Lines 36 and 37 declare **sMessage**—the character array that contains the text we display in the message box—and construct **s**—the **ostrstream** we use to write to **sMessage**. Because check box states are independent of each other, we must get the state of each individual check box. Line 40

```
int nChocolate = GetButtonStatus( IDC_CHOCOLATE );
```

assigns **nChocolate** the **int** returned from **GetButtonStatus** when **GetButtonStatus** is passed **IDC_CHOCOLATE** (i.e., the dialog identifier for the **Chocolate** check box defined on line 82). Function **GetButtonStatus** returns an integer representing the state of a check box. We will discuss this function momentarily. Lines 41 and 42 call **GetButtonStatus** to check the state of the **Vanilla** and **Strawberry** check boxes, respectively. Lines 44 through 60 write the appropriate strings (based upon the values **nChocolate**, **nStrawberry** and **nVanilla** that represent the state of the three check boxes) to **str** and display **sMessage**'s contents in a message box.

Function **GetButtonStatus** (line 27) is called from message handler **OnOk**. The statement (line 29)

```
CButton *pCButton = ( CButton * ) GetDlgItem( nId );
```

gets a pointer to the check box corresponding to the identifier stored in **nId** (e.g., **IDC_CHOCOLATE**). The pointer returned by **GetDlgItem** is cast from **CWnd *** to **CButton *** because **nId** corresponds to a check box and a check box is a **CButton**.

Line 30

```
return pCButton->GetCheck();
```

calls function *GetCheck* to get the check box's state. Function **GetCheck** returns **0** if the check box is not selected and returns **1** if the check box is selected.

Lines 63 through 65 define the message map for **CCheckBoxDialog**. Message identifier **IDOK** (predefined by MFC) is mapped to message handler **OnOK**. Lines 69 through 78 create an instance of our Win32 application.

The resource file (line 85) contains our **DIALOG** description for **CCheckBox**. Line 93

```
GROUPBOX      "Flavors",      IDC_STATIC,      15, 5, 80, 50
```

is the resource statement for the **GROUPBOX** titled **Flavors**. A **GROUPBOX** does not generate messages, so we give it the **IDC_STATIC** identifier. The only purpose of the **GROUPBOX** is to visually indicate that a group of controls are related. The **GROUPBOX** caption (**"Flavors"**) is the name displayed by the group box on the GUI.

Lines 95 through 97

```
AUTOCHECKBOX "Chocolate",  IDC_CHOCOLATE,  20, 15, 60, 10
AUTOCHECKBOX "Vanilla"  ,  IDC_VANILLA,    20, 25, 60, 10
AUTOCHECKBOX "Strawberry", IDC_STRAWBERRY, 20, 35, 60, 10
```

are the resource statements for the three check boxes (**AUTOCHECKBOX**es). Each check box is given a caption (e.g., **"Chocolate"**, etc.), a programmer-defined dialog ID (e.g., **IDC_CHOCOLATE**, etc.), a coordinate set [e.g., *(20, 15)*, etc.] and a width and height (e.g., 60-by-10 dialog units).

4.4 Radio Buttons

Like check boxes, *radio buttons* are state controls (i.e., on/off or true/false). Radio buttons are round and only one radio button in a group can be true; and selecting one radio button forces all other radio buttons in the group to be false. When selected, a radio button has a solid circle in its center. Unlike check boxes, radio buttons are almost always grouped with a group box. The **AUTORADIOBUTTON** statement in the resource file is used to create a radio button.

Look-and-Feel Observation 4.3

Radio buttons present the user with mutually exclusive choices from a group of items. At any moment, only one radio button in a group can have a checked state.

Figure 4.3 demonstrates creating and using radio buttons in an application. In this example we modify Fig. 4.2 to use radio buttons rather than check boxes. We also add a second set of radio buttons that allows the user to choose **Cone** or **Cup**.

The **CRadioButtonDialog** class definition (line 4) consists of four **private** members—character pointers **m_lpszFlavor** and **m_lpszContainer**, character array **m_szOrder** and macro **DECLARE_MESSAGE_MAP()**—and two **public** member functions—a constructor and a message handler. The constructor (line 7) invokes the base-class constructor and initializes data members **m_lpszFlavor** and **m_lpsz-Container** to the null string.

Message handler **OnOk** (line 27) is called when the **OK** button is clicked. Line 30

```
int nFlavor = GetCheckedRadioButton( IDC_CHOCOLATE,
                                      IDC_STRAWBERRY );
```

calls **CWnd** member function *GetCheckedRadioButton* to determine which (if any) radio button in the group beginning with **IDC_CHOCOLATE** (defined on line 80) and ending with **IDC_STRAWBERRY** (defined on line 82) is selected. We will discuss how groups of radio buttons are specified when we discuss the resource file (lines 86 through 106). The value returned by **GetCheckedRadioButton** is the dialog identifier (e.g., **IDC_CHOCOLATE**) for the selected radio button or **0** if none is selected. This value is assigned to **nFlavor**.

```
1   // Fig. 4.3: CRadioButtonDialog.h
2   // radio button example
3
4   class CRadioButtonDialog : public CDialog
5   {
6   public:
7      CRadioButtonDialog( char *lpszName )
8         : CDialog( lpszName ), m_lpszFlavor( "" ),
9           m_lpszContainer( "" ) {}
10
11     afx_msg void OnOK();      // clicked the "OK" button
12
13  private:
14     char *m_lpszFlavor;
15     char *m_lpszContainer;
16     char m_szOrder[ 64 ];
17
18     DECLARE_MESSAGE_MAP()
19  };
```

Fig. 4.3   Creating and using radio buttons (part 1 of 6).

```
20  // Fig. 4.3: radiobutton.cpp
21  // radio button example
22  #include <afxwin.h>
23  #include "radiobutton_ids.h"
24  #include "CRadioButtonDialog.h"
25
26  // clicked the "OK" button
27  afx_msg void CRadioButtonDialog::OnOK()
28  {
29     // get flavor ID of selected radiobutton from group
30     int nFlavor = GetCheckedRadioButton( IDC_CHOCOLATE,
31                                          IDC_STRAWBERRY );
32     switch ( nFlavor ) {
33        case IDC_CHOCOLATE:
34           m_lpszFlavor = "Chocolate";
35           break;
36        case IDC_STRAWBERRY:
37           m_lpszFlavor = "Strawberry";
38           break;
39        default:
40           m_lpszFlavor = "Vanilla";
41     }
42
43     // get container ID of selected radiobutton from group
44     int nContainer = GetCheckedRadioButton( IDC_CONE,
45                                             IDC_CUP );
46     switch ( nContainer ) {
47        case IDC_CONE:
48           m_lpszContainer = "Cone";
49           break;
```

Fig. 4.3   Creating and using radio buttons (part 2 of 6).

```
50          default:
51              m_lpszContainer = "Cup";
52      }
53
54      // concatenate the flavor and container in a string
55      strcpy( m_szOrder, m_lpszFlavor );
56      strcat( m_szOrder, " " );
57      strcat( m_szOrder, m_lpszContainer );
58
59      MessageBox( m_szOrder, "Ice Cream Order:" );
60  }
61
62  BEGIN_MESSAGE_MAP( CRadioButtonDialog, CDialog )
63      ON_COMMAND( IDOK, OnOK )
64  END_MESSAGE_MAP()
65
66  // start application, create dialog window
67  class CRadioButtonApp : public CWinApp
68  {
69  public:
70      BOOL InitInstance()
71      {
72          CRadioButtonDialog radioButtonDialog( "CRadioButton" );
73          radioButtonDialog.DoModal();   // run dialog window
74          return FALSE;                  // exit
75      }
76
77  } radioButtonApp;
```

Fig. 4.3   Creating and using radio buttons (part 3 of 6).

```
78  // Fig. 4.3: radiobutton_ids.h
79  // radio button message identifiers
80  #define IDC_CHOCOLATE   2200
81  #define IDC_VANILLA     2201
82  #define IDC_STRAWBERRY  2202
83
84  #define IDC_CONE        2210
85  #define IDC_CUP         2211
```

Fig. 4.3   Creating and using radio buttons (part 4 of 6).

A **switch** structure (line 32) determines which dialog identifier **nFlavor** is equivalent to and assigns the appropriate string to **m_lpszFlavor**. For this example, **IDC_VANILLA** (defined on line 81) is the default. Exercise 4.8 asks for this example to be modified to require a flavor selection.

Line 44 calls **GetCheckedRadioButton** to determine which (if any) are selected from the radio button group containing **IDC_CONE** (defined on line 84) and **IDC_CUP** (defined on line 85). The dialog identifier returned is assigned to **nContainer**. A **switch** structure (line 46) assigns the appropriate string to **m_lpszContainer**. Lines 55 through 57 build the string **m_szOrder** by calling function **strcat**. Function **MessageBox** is called on line 59 to display **m_szOrder**.

```
86   // Fig. 4.3: radiobutton.rc
87   // radio button resource file
88   #include <afxres.h>
89   #include "radiobutton_ids.h"
90
91   CRadioButton DIALOG  50, 50, 115, 130
92   CAPTION "Radio Button Example"
93   {
94      GROUPBOX          "Flavors",     IDC_STATIC,    15, 10, 80, 50
95      AUTORADIOBUTTON "Chocolate",   IDC_CHOCOLATE, 20, 20, 60, 10,
96                                     WS_GROUP
97      AUTORADIOBUTTON "Vanilla",     IDC_VANILLA,   20, 30, 60, 10
98      AUTORADIOBUTTON "Strawberry",  IDC_STRAWBERRY,20, 40, 60, 10
99
100     GROUPBOX          "Container",   IDC_STATIC,    15, 60, 80, 40
101     AUTORADIOBUTTON "Cone",        IDC_CONE,      20, 70, 60, 10,
102                                     WS_GROUP
103     AUTORADIOBUTTON "Cup",         IDC_CUP,       20, 80, 60, 10
104
105     DEFPUSHBUTTON     "OK",          IDOK,          40,105, 30, 15
106  }
```

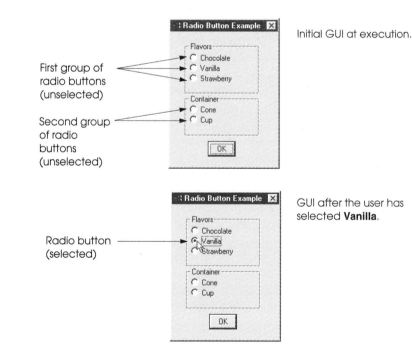

Fig. 4.3   Creating and using radio buttons (part 5 of 6).

Lines 62 through 64 define the message map for **CRadioButtonDialog**. Message identifier **IDOK** (predefined by Windows) is mapped to message handler **OnOK**. Lines 67 through 77 create an instance of our Win32 application.

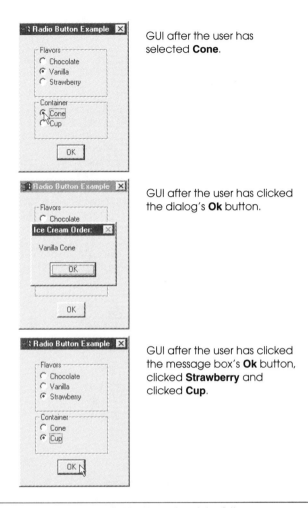

GUI after the user has selected **Cone**.

GUI after the user has clicked the dialog's **Ok** button.

GUI after the user has clicked the message box's **Ok** button, clicked **Strawberry** and clicked **Cup**.

Fig. 4.3   Creating and using radio buttons (part 6 of 6).

The resource file (line 86) contains our **DIALOG** description for **CRadioButton**. Lines 94 through 98

```
GROUPBOX           "Flavors",     IDC_STATIC,     15, 10, 80, 50
AUTORADIOBUTTON "Chocolate",   IDC_CHOCOLATE, 20, 20, 60, 10,
                               WS_GROUP
AUTORADIOBUTTON "Vanilla"  ,   IDC_VANILLA,    20, 30, 60, 10
AUTORADIOBUTTON "Strawberry",  IDC_STRAWBERRY, 20, 40, 60, 10
```

create a **GROUPBOX** and three radio buttons (*AUTORADIOBUTTON*s). Each radio button is given a caption (e.g., **"Chocolate"**), a dialog identifier (e.g., **IDC_CHOCOLATE**), a set of coordinates, a width and a height. Window style *WS_GROUP* indicates that **IDC_CHOCOLATE** is the first radio button in a group. Constant **WS_GROUP** distinguishes different groups of controls—not a **GROUPBOX**. In this example, we have two radio button groups—one for the flavor and one for the container. The radio button group for the flavor begins with **IDC_CHOCOLATE** and ends with **IDC_STAWBERRY** because **IDC_CONE** (lines 101 and 102) uses **WS_GROUP** to indicate the beginning of a new radio button group.

4.5 List Boxes

List box controls display a list of items (as strings) from which the user can select one or more items. A *single-selection list* allows the user to select one item at a time. A *multiple-selection list* allows the user to select any number of items. We demonstrate how to create and use single-selection list boxes (defined with class ***CListBox***). Each string in the list box has a unique integer *index*. The first item in the list has index zero. The program of Fig. 4.4 allows the user to copy food items from one list box into another.

The **CListBoxDialog** class definition (line 4) contains two **private** members— a **static** array of pointers to characters named **s_alpszChoices** and macro **DECLARE_MESSAGE_MAP()**—and four **public** member functions—a constructor, a function and two message handlers. The constructor (line 6) invokes the base-class constructor. The **static** array **s_alpszChoices** is initialized on line 68 using the initializer syntax for **static** class members. This data is **static** because one instance can be shared by all members of the class. For information on **static** class members, see Section 7.7 of *C++ How to Program: Second Edition.*

Lines 24 overrides function ***OnInitDialog*** to initialize the dialog box. Function **OnInitDialog** is called by MFC when **DoModal** (line 82) is called. To ensure proper initialization of all the inherited properties and behaviors, we call the base-class version of **OnInitDialog** on line 27. Lines 30 and 31

```
CListBox *pChoices;
pChoices = ( CListBox * ) GetDlgItem( IDC_CHOICES );
```

declare **pChoices** as a **CListBox** pointer and assign **pChoices** the address of the list box named **IDC_CHOICES** (defined on line 90). The **CWnd *** returned by **GetDlgItem** is cast to derived-class type **CListBox ***.

```
1   // Fig. 4.4: CListBoxDialog.h
2   // list box control example
3
4   class CListBoxDialog : public CDialog {
5   public:
6      CListBoxDialog( char *lpszName ) : CDialog( lpszName ) {}
7
8      BOOL OnInitDialog();
9
10     afx_msg void OnAdd();
11     afx_msg void OnClear();
12
13  private:
14     static char *s_alpszChoices[];
15
16     DECLARE_MESSAGE_MAP()
17  };
```

Fig. 4.4   Creating and using a list box (part 1 of 7).

```
18  // Fig. 4.4: listbox.cpp
19  // list box control example
20  #include <afxwin.h>
21  #include "listbox_ids.h"
22  #include "CListBoxDialog.h"
23
24  BOOL CListBoxDialog::OnInitDialog()
25  {
26     // call base class initialization first
27     CDialog::OnInitDialog();
28
29     // Get address of List Box
30     CListBox *pChoices;
31     pChoices = ( CListBox * ) GetDlgItem( IDC_CHOICES );
32
33     // add items to list box
34     for ( int i = 0; s_alpszChoices[ i ] != NULL; i++ )
35        pChoices->AddString( s_alpszChoices[ i ] );
36
37     return TRUE;
38  }
39
40  // clicked the "Add" button
41  afx_msg void CListBoxDialog::OnAdd()
42  {
43     CListBox *pChoices;
44     pChoices = ( CListBox *) GetDlgItem( IDC_CHOICES );
45
46     int iCurSel = pChoices->GetCurSel();
47
48     if ( iCurSel == LB_ERR ) {
49        MessageBox( "Select an item.", "Choices",
50                    MB_ICONWARNING );
51        return;
52     }
53
54     CListBox *pSelected;
55     pSelected = ( CListBox * ) GetDlgItem( IDC_SELECTED );
56     char szText[ 32 ];
57     pChoices->GetText( iCurSel, szText );
58     pSelected->AddString( szText );
59  }
60
61  afx_msg void CListBoxDialog::OnClear()
62  {
63     CListBox *pSelected;
64     pSelected = ( CListBox * ) GetDlgItem( IDC_SELECTED );
65     pSelected->ResetContent();      // clear list box
66  }
67
68  char *CListBoxDialog::s_alpszChoices[]
69        = { "Chicken", "Fish", "Salad", NULL };
70
```

Fig. 4.4   Creating and using a list box (part 2 of 7).

```
71  BEGIN_MESSAGE_MAP( CListBoxDialog, CDialog )
72     ON_COMMAND( IDC_ADD,   OnAdd )
73     ON_COMMAND( IDC_CLEAR, OnClear )
74  END_MESSAGE_MAP()
75
76
77  class CListBoxApp : public CWinApp {
78  public:
79     BOOL InitInstance()
80     {
81        CListBoxDialog listBoxDialog( "ListBoxDialog" );
82        listBoxDialog.DoModal();   // returns IDOK or IDCANCEL
83        return FALSE;
84     }
85
86  } listBoxApp;
```

Fig. 4.4   Creating and using a list box (part 3 of 7).

```
87  // Fig. 4.4: listbox_ids.h
88  // listbox message ID definitions
89
90  #define IDC_CHOICES  2101
91  #define IDC_SELECTED 2102
92
93  #define IDC_ADD      2103
94  #define IDC_CLEAR    2104
```

Fig. 4.4   Creating and using a list box (part 4 of 7).

```
95   // Fig 4.4: listbox.rc
96   // ListBox resource file
97
98   #include "afxres.h"
99   #include "listbox_ids.h"
100
101  ListBoxDialog DIALOG   20, 20, 132, 150
102  CAPTION "List Box Example"
103  {
104      LTEXT          "Choices:", IDC_STATIC,  30,   5, 50,   8
105      LISTBOX        IDC_CHOICES,             30,  15  68,  48
106
107      DEFPUSHBUTTON "Add", IDC_ADD,           50,  54, 32,  16
108
109      LTEXT          "Selected:", IDC_STATIC, 30,  80  50,   8
110      LISTBOX        IDC_SELECTED,            30,  90  68,  48,
111                     WS_VSCROLL
112
113      PUSHBUTTON     "Clear",  IDC_CLEAR,     50, 130, 30,  15
114  }
```

Fig. 4.4   Creating and using a list box (part 5 of 7).

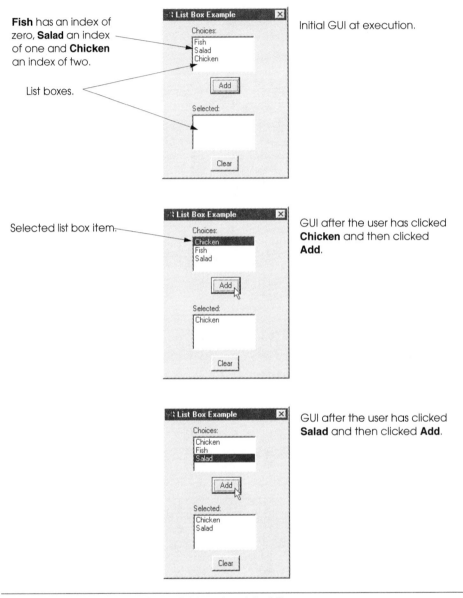

Fish has an index of zero, **Salad** an index of one and **Chicken** an index of two.

List boxes.

Initial GUI at execution.

Selected list box item.

GUI after the user has clicked **Chicken** and then clicked **Add**.

GUI after the user has clicked **Salad** and then clicked **Add**.

Fig. 4.4   Creating and using a list box (part 6 of 7).

The **for** loop (line 34) calls function ***AddString*** to add each string in **s_alpszChoices** to the **CListBox** pointed to by **pChoices**. Because we did not call **setFocus** to set the focus for a specific control, **TRUE** is returned to allow Windows to set the focus to the first control in the tab order.

Message handler **OnAdd** (line 41) is called when the **Add** button is clicked. Line 44 gets a pointer, **pChoices**, to the **IDC_CHOICES** list box, and line 46

```
int iCurSel = pChoices->GetCurSel();
```

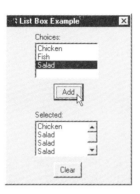

GUI after the user has clicked **Salad** and then clicked **Add** repeatedly.

Fig. 4.4 Creating and using a list box (part 7 of 7).

calls function *GetCurSel* to get the index for the currently selected list box item. If no items are selected, **GetCurSel** returns the constant value *LB_ERR*. The **if** (line 48) tests for **LB_ERR** and displays a message box and exits the function if an item is not selected.

Line 55 gets a pointer, **pSelected**, to the **IDC_SELECTED** (defined on line 91) list box. Line 56 declares a temporary array (**szText**) that is used to store the string selected in the **IDC_CHOICES** list box. Line 57

```
pChoices->GetText( iCurSel, szText );
```

calls **CListBox** member function *GetText* to get the string at **iCurSel** index from the **CListBox** object pointed to by **pChoices** and store the string in **szText**. The string in **szText** is added to the list box pointed to by **pSelected** with a call to **AddString**.

Message handler **OnClear** (line 61) is called when the **Clear** button is clicked. Message handler **OnClear** gets a pointer to the **IDC_SELECTED** list box and calls **CListBox** member function *ResetContent* to remove all items from the list box.

Lines 71 through 74 define the message map for **CListBoxDialog**. Message identifier **IDC_ADD** (defined on line 93) is mapped to message handler **OnAdd** and message identifier **IDC_CLEAR** (defined on line 94) is mapped to message handler **OnClear**. Lines 77 through 86 create an instance of our Win32 application.

The resource file (lines 95 through 114) contains our **DIALOG** description for **List-BoxDialog**. Line 105 uses the resource definition language to create a *LISTBOX* with the identifier **IDC_CHOICES**. Line 110 creates **LISTBOX IDC_SELECTED**. Windows style **WS_VSCROLL** indicates that the **IDC_SELECTED** list box will have a vertical scroll bar if the list box contains more items than the list box can display.

4.6 Combo Boxes

A *combo box* is a control that combines the features of an edit text control with a list box. Like a list box, a combo box presents a list of items (as strings) from which the user can select an item. Unlike a list box, a combo box does not display its list of items until the user clicks the combo box's *down arrow* (see Fig. 4.4). When a combo box item is selected (by clicking with the mouse), the selected item is displayed in the combo box's *text area* (i.e., the part of the combo box that resembles an edit text control). MFC class *CComboBox* encapsulates the functionality for a combo box. The first item in a combo box has index zero.

Figure 4.5 is similar to Fig. 4.4 except that we use a combo box instead of a list box to display the available food item choices.

```
1   // Fig. 4.5: CComboBoxDialog.h
2   // combo box control example
3
4   class CComboBoxDialog : public CDialog {
5   public:
6      CComboBoxDialog( char *lpszName ) : CDialog( lpszName ) {}
7
8      BOOL OnInitDialog();
9      afx_msg void OnAdd();      // clicked the "Add" button
10     afx_msg void OnClear();    // clicked the "Clear" button
11
12  private:
13     static char *s_alpszChoices[];
14
15     DECLARE_MESSAGE_MAP()
16  };
```

Fig. 4.5   Creating and using a combo box (part 1 of 7).

```
17  // Fig. 4.5: combobox.cpp
18  // combo box control example
19  #include <afxwin.h>
20  #include "combobox_ids.h"
21  #include "CComboBoxDialog.h"
22
23  BOOL CComboBoxDialog::OnInitDialog()
24  {
25     CDialog::OnInitDialog();
26     CComboBox *pChoices;
27     pChoices = ( CComboBox * ) GetDlgItem( IDC_CHOICES );
28
29     // add strings to combo box
30     for ( int i = 0; s_alpszChoices[ i ] != NULL; i++ )
31        pChoices->AddString( s_alpszChoices[ i ] );
32
33     return TRUE;
34  }
35
36  // clicked the "Add" button
37  afx_msg void CComboBoxDialog::OnAdd()
38  {
39     CComboBox *pChoices;
40     pChoices = ( CComboBox * ) GetDlgItem( IDC_CHOICES );
41
42     int iCurSel = pChoices->GetCurSel();
43
```

Fig. 4.5   Creating and using a combo box (part 2 of 7).

```
44     if ( iCurSel == CB_ERR ) {
45         MessageBox( "Select an item.", "Choices",
46                     MB_ICONWARNING );
47         return;
48     }
49
50     char lpszText[ 32 ];
51     pChoices->GetLBText( iCurSel, lpszText );
52
53     CListBox *pSelected =
54             ( CListBox * ) GetDlgItem( IDC_SELECTED );
55     pSelected->AddString( lpszText );
56 }
57
58
59 afx_msg void CComboBoxDialog::OnClear()
60 {
61     CListBox *pSelected =
62             ( CListBox * ) GetDlgItem( IDC_SELECTED );
63     pSelected->ResetContent();    // clear list box
64 }
65
66 char *CComboBoxDialog::s_alpszChoices[]
67     = { "Chicken", "Fish", "Salad", NULL };
68
69 BEGIN_MESSAGE_MAP( CComboBoxDialog, CDialog )
70     ON_COMMAND( IDC_ADD,   OnAdd )
71     ON_COMMAND( IDC_CLEAR, OnClear )
72 END_MESSAGE_MAP()
73
74
75 class CComboBoxApp : public CWinApp {
76 public:
77     BOOL InitInstance()
78     {
79         CComboBoxDialog comboBoxDialog( "ComboBoxDialog" );
80         comboBoxDialog.DoModal();    // returns IDOK or IDCANCEL
81         return FALSE;                // exit
82     }
83
84 } comboBoxApp;
```

Fig. 4.5   Creating and using a combo box (part 3 of 7).

```
85 // Fig. 4.5: combobox_ids.h
86 // combo box message identifiers
87
88 #define IDC_CHOICES  2101
89 #define IDC_ADD      2102
90 #define IDC_SELECTED 2103
91 #define IDC_CLEAR    2104
```

Fig. 4.5   Creating and using a combo box (part 4 of 7).

```
92   // Fig 4.5: combobox.rc
93   // combo box resource file
94   #include <afxres.h>
95   #include "combobox_ids.h"
96
97   ComboBoxDialog DIALOG 20, 20, 132, 150
98   CAPTION "Combo Box Example"
99   {
100      LTEXT          "Choices:", IDC_STATIC,  30,   5, 50,  8
101      COMBOBOX       IDC_CHOICES,             30,  15, 68, 48,
102                     CBS_SORT | CBS_DROPDOWNLIST
103
104      DEFPUSHBUTTON "Add", IDC_ADD,           50,  54, 30, 15
105
106      LTEXT          "Selected:", IDC_STATIC, 30,  80, 50,  8
107      LISTBOX        IDC_SELECTED,            30,  90, 68, 48,
108                     WS_VSCROLL
109
110      PUSHBUTTON     "Clear",  IDC_CLEAR,     50, 130, 30, 15
111   }
```

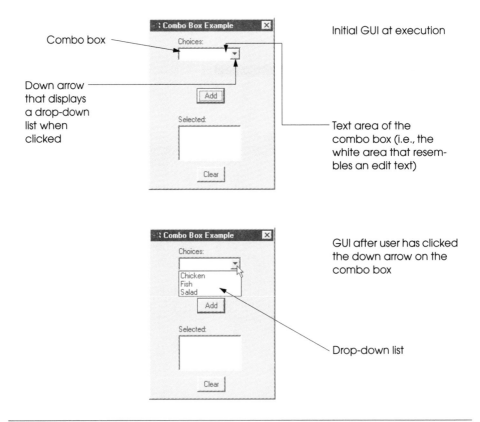

Fig. 4.5   Creating and using a combo box (part 5 of 7).

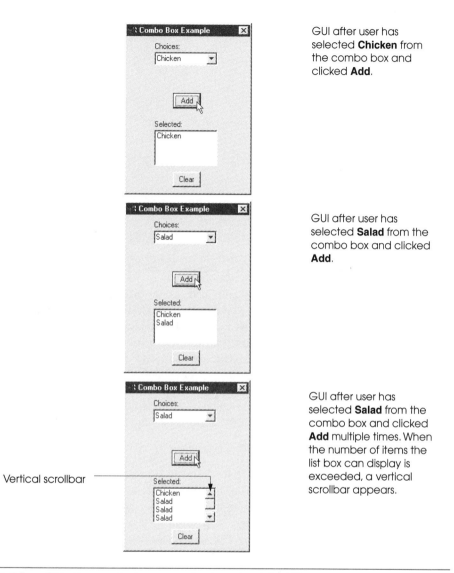

GUI after user has
selected **Chicken** from
the combo box and
clicked **Add**.

GUI after user has
selected **Salad** from the
combo box and clicked
Add.

GUI after user has
selected **Salad** from the
combo box and clicked
Add multiple times. When
the number of items the
list box can display is
exceeded, a vertical
scrollbar appears.

Vertical scrollbar

Fig. 4.5   Creating and using a combo box (part 6 of 7).

The **CComboBoxDialog** class definition (line 4) contains two **private** members—a **static** array of pointers to characters named **s_alpszChoices** and macro **DECLARE_MESSAGE_MAP()**—and four **public** member functions—a constructor, a function and two message handlers. The constructor (line 6) invokes the base-class constructor. The **static** array **s_alpszChoices** is initialized on lines 66 and 67 using the initializer syntax for **static** class members.

Line 23 overrides function **OnInitDialog** to initialize the dialog box. Function **OnInitDialog** is called when the **CDialog** function **DoModal** (line 80) is called. To ensure proper initialization, we call the base-class version of **OnInitDialog** on line 25. Lines 26 and 27

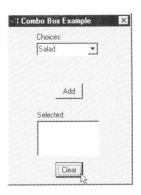

GUI after user has clicked
Clear.

Fig. 4.5 Creating and using a combo box (part 7 of 7).

```
CComboBox *pChoices;
pChoices = ( CComboBox * ) GetDlgItem( IDC_CHOICES );
```

declare **pChoices** as a **CComboBox** pointer and assigns **pChoices** the address of the list box named **IDC_CHOICES** (defined on line 88). The **CWnd *** returned by **GetDlgItem** is cast to **CComboBox *** so that we can call **CComboBox** specific methods.

The **for** loop (line 30) calls **CComboBox** member function **AddString** to add each string in **s_alpszChoices** to the **CComboBox** pointed to by **pChoices**. Because we did not call **setFocus** to set the focus for a specific control, **TRUE** is returned to allow Windows to set the focus to the first control in the tab order.

Message handler **OnAdd** (line 37) is called when the **Add** button is clicked. Line 40 gets a pointer, **pChoices**, to the **IDC_CHOICES** combo box, and line 42

```
int iCurSel = pChoices->GetCurSel();
```

calls **CComboBox** function **GetCurSel** to get the index for the combo box item that is currently selected. If an item is not selected, **GetCurSel** returns the constant value **CB_ERR**. The **if** (line 44) tests for **CB_ERR**. If true, a message box is displayed and the function is exited.

Line 50 declares a temporary array that is used to store the string selected in the **IDC_CHOICES** combo box. Line 51

```
pChoices->GetLBText( iCurSel, lpszText );
```

calls function *GetLBText* to get the string at **iCurSel** index from the **CComboBox** object to which **pChoices** points. The selected item is stored in the argument **lpszText**.

Lines 53 and 54 get a pointer, **pSelected**, to the **IDC_SELECTED** (defined on line 90) list box. The string in **lpszText** is added to the list box pointed to by **pSelected** with a call to **AddString**.

Message handler **OnClear** (line 59) is called when the **Clear** button is clicked. Message handler **OnClear** gets a pointer to the **IDC_SELECTED** list box and calls function **ResetContent** to remove all items from the list box.

Lines 69 through 72 define the message map for **CListBoxDialog**. Message identifier **IDC_ADD** (defined on line 89) is mapped to message handler **OnAdd**, and message identifier **IDC_CLEAR** (defined on line 91) is mapped to message handler **OnClear**. Lines 75 through 84 create an instance of our Win32 application.

The resource file (line 92) contains our **DIALOG** description for **ComboBoxDialog**. Line 101 creates a **COMBOBOX** with the identifier **IDC_CHOICES**. Combo box style **CBS_SORT** indicates that the combo box is to maintain its list of items in sorted order at all times and **CBS_DROPDOWNLIST** indicates that the GUI for the combo box is a drop-down style (i.e., displays a down arrow).

Summary

- An edit text control (also called an edit box) is a rectangular area where text can be input or displayed. Edit text controls can be single-line controls or multiline controls.
- Style **ES_MULTILINE** indicates that an **EDITTEXT** is multiline.
- Style **WS_VSCROLL** indicates that a control should have a vertical scrollbar.
- Horizontal dialog units are 1/4 the typical character width of the current font and vertical dialog units are 1/8 the typical character height.
- Check boxes are controls that present the user with boolean choices (i.e., true or false, yes or no, on or off). If checked, the choice is selected (i.e., true) and if unchecked the choice is not selected (i.e., false). Check boxes behave independent of other check boxes. The **AUTOCHECKBOX** statement in the resource file is used to create a check box.
- **GROUPBOX**es are static controls that visually indicate a group of related controls.
- **CButton** member function **GetCheck** returns a check box's state.
- Radio buttons are state controls (i.e., on/off or true/false). Radio buttons appear round in the user interface and are mutually exclusive of other radio buttons in the same group. The **AUTORAD-IOBUTTON** statement in the resource file is used to create a radio button.
- **CWnd** member function **GetCheckedRadioButton** determines which (if any) radio button in a group is selected.
- Style **WS_GROUP** indicates the beginning of a radio button group.
- List box controls display a list of items (as strings) from which the user can select one or more items. MFC class **CListBox** encapsulates the functionality for a list box. Each string in the list box has associated with it a unique number called an index. The first item in the list has index zero.
- **CDialog** function **OnInitDialog** initializes a dialog box.
- **CListBox** member function **AddString** adds strings to a list box.
- **CListBox** member function **GetCurSel** gets the index for the selected list box item. If an item is not selected, **GetCurSel** returns the constant value **LB_ERR**.
- **CListBox** member function **GetText** returns the string at a specific list box index.
- **CListBox** member function **ResetContent** removes all items from a list box.
- A combo box is a control that combines the features of an edit text control with a list box. Like a list box, a combo box presents a list of items from which the user can select an item. Unlike a list box, a combo box can have the **CBS_DROPDOWN** or **CBS_DROPDOWNLIST** styles that hide the list of items until the user clicks the combo box's down arrow. When a combo box item is selected, the selected item is displayed in the combo box's text area. MFC class **CComboBox** encapsulates the functionality for a combo box. The first item in a combo box has an index of zero.
- **CComboBox** member function **GetLBText** returns the string at the specified combo box index.
- Combo box style **CBS_SORT** indicates that the combo box is to maintain a sorted list of items, and **CBS_DROPDOWNLIST** indicates that the GUI for the combo box is a drop-down style.

Terminology

AddString function of class **CComboBox**
AddString function of class **CListBox**
AUTOCHECKBOX resource statement
AUTORADIOBUTTON resource statement
CB_ERR constant
CBS_DROPDOWNLIST combo box style
CBS_SORT combo box style
CComboBox class
CEdit class
check box
CListBox class
combo box
COMBOBOX resource statement
container
DIALOG resource statement
down arrow of a combo box
drop-down list of a combo box
edit box control
edit text control
ES_MULTILINE edit style
ES_WANTRETURN edit style
frame
GetCheck member function of class **CButton**
GetCheckedRadioButton function of **CWnd**
GetCurSel function of class **CComboBox**
GetCurSel function of class **CListBox**
GetLBText function of class **CComboBox**
GetText function of class **CListBox**

group box
GROUPBOX resource statement
horizontal dialog unit
index
LB_ERR constant
LBS_NOTIFY list box style
LBS_SORT list box style
list box
LISTBOX resource statement
MB_ICONWARNING constant
multiline edit text control
multiple-selection list
OnInitDialog function of class **CDialog**
radio button
ResetContent function of class **CComboBox**
ResetContent function of class **CListBox**
scrollbar
selected item
SetFocus function of class **CWnd**
single-line controls
single-selection list
static controls
text area of a combo box
vertical dialog unit
vertical scrollbar
WS_GROUP window style
WS_VSCROLL window style

Look-and-Feel Observations

4.1   Check boxes present the user with choices from a group of items. At any time multiple check boxes can be selected.

4.2   Use a group box to enclose a number of related controls. Logical groupings make a dialog box easier for the user to understand.

4.3   Radio buttons present the user with mutually exclusive choices from a group of items. At any moment, only one radio button in a group can have a selected state.

Software Engineering Observation

4.1   Dialog units make it easy to scale GUI controls to text. If you want a control that is 8 characters wide and 2 characters high, a 32-by-16 dialog units box will do.

Self-Review Exercises

4.1   Fill in the blanks in each of the following:
   a) Style _____ specifies that an **EDITTEXT** holds multiple lines of text.
   b) Style _____ specifies that a **LISTBOX** has a vertical scrollbar.
   c) A _____ is a combination of an edit text control and a list box control.
   d) Style _____ indicates that a combo box should sort its items.
   e) Function _____ adds a string to a **CListBox**.

4.2   State whether each of the following is *true* or *false*. If *false*, explain why.

a) Mutually exclusive options are implemented using check boxes.

b) Function **GetCheck** returns the state of a check box or a radio button.

c) **SetWindowText** requires either **'\r'** or **'\n'** to force a new line in a window.

d) **LB_ERR** indicates that no items were selected in a list box.

Answers to Self-Review Exercises

4.1   a) **ES_MULTILINE**. b) **WS_VSCROLL**. c) combo box. d) **CBS_SORT**. e) **AddString**.

4.2   a) False. It is radio buttons that allow only one in a group to be set at a time.

b) True.

c) False. Both **'\r'** and **'\n'** are required to force a new line in a window.

d) True.

Exercises

4.3   Modify Fig. 4.4 so that the **Choices** and **Selected** list boxes are side-by-side with the **Add** button between them. Below the **Add** button, place a **Delete** button to remove an item from the **Selected** list. Find the function to delete an entry in a list box near the online documentation for the function to add an entry. Change the main application window title and the dialog title to be more meaningful to the application. Your solution should look similar to the following window:

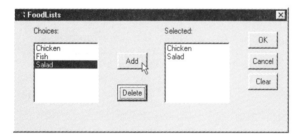

4.4   Modify Exercise 4.3 to use a combo box rather than the left list box.

4.5   Use two multiline edit box controls to make a simple message send and receive program. After the user types text in one edit box control and clicks a **Send** button, your program displays the text in the other edit box control.

4.6   Continue to extend your application derived from the menu example. Modify your solution to Exercises 2.7 through 2.9 or 3.3 through 3.6 to use radio buttons and check boxes.

4.7   Modify your solution to Exercise 4.6 to display selected items in a list box.

4.8   Modify Figure 4.3 to display a message box "**Please select a flavor.**", if the user does not select a flavor. Display a similar message if the user does not select a container. Add two more **Flavors** and a new **Container** option "Bowl".

5

MFC Graphics

Objectives

- To understand MFC graphics concepts.
- To be able to draw various graphical shapes such as circles and rectangles.
- To be able to set line color, thickness and pattern.
- To be able to set colors and patterns for filled areas.
- To be able to use a timer.
- To be able to display an image.
- To be able to use fonts.

One picture is worth ten thousand words.
Chinese proverb

Treat nature in terms of the cylinder, the sphere, the cone, all in perspective.
Paul Cézanne

Nothing ever becomes real till it is experienced—even a proverb is no proverb to you till your life has illustrated it.
John Keats

Capture its reality in paint!
Paul Cézanne

Outline

5.1 Introduction

MFC programs implement a graphical user interface with menus and dialog boxes containing various controls, from buttons to combo boxes. These are navigational tools to find information or to request some action. An application program can be built entirely with existing controls as our previous examples have shown or can present information in a format not available using existing controls. For this we must write code to draw in a window. This chapter explores how to display information on the screen graphically. We can draw shapes, display pictures and write text controlling the font, size and color of the text. We basically have control over every pixel on the screen. At the lowest level MFC has **Set-Pixel** and **GetPixel** functions to set and get the RGB color values for individual pixels. There are also many higher-level functions for drawing lines and shapes that simplify graphics programming.

An MFC device context provides the functions for drawing and contains the data members that keep track of the *bitmap* (an array representing the pixels of an image), *pen* (an object for drawing lines of a specified color, thickness and pattern), *brush* (an object for filling enclosed regions with a specified color and pattern) and *color palette* (an object containing available colors). The device context simplifies MFC programming by encapsulating (i.e. hiding details of) the Windows *graphical device interface* (*GDI*) objects and functions. When a function in a window class needs to draw in that window, it creates a **CClientDC** object to write in the client area of the window. The function **OnPaint** for a window creates a **CPaintDC** object to access the region of the window that needs to be updated. The **CPaintDC** constructor calls function ***BeginPaint*** and the destructor calls function ***EndPaint***, encapsulating some Windows GDI function calls that acquire and release the GDI resources for the MFC programmer. In our examples we redraw the entire window but there are techniques for selectively drawing only the changing regions of a window. Our examples are simple and do not require these optimizations.

5.2 Coordinate Systems

The image displayed on the screen is composed of thousands of *pixels* (picture elements). Each pixel has a color and a physical position or address on the screen. A *coordinate system* defines the origin (location of position *0,0*), the orientation (whether incrementing *y* goes up or down the screen) and scale units (pixels or other measurement), etc. The coordinate system can be chosen to match the application program's logic. Two types of measurements are available. *Device units* are physical pixels or dots counted from left to right and top to bottom of the screen (or other device). *Logical units* are counted relative to the top-left corner of a window. *Logical units* can be pixels (the default), English (1/100th or 1/1000th of an inch) or metric (1/10th or 1/100th of a millimeter) units. Logical units are usually the same in both the horizontal and vertical dimensions but can be scaled for higher or lower resolution in the horizontal or vertical directions. Dialog units are a type of logical unit used for dialog windows. Horizontal dialog units are 1/4 the width of the average current font character. Vertical dialog units are 1/8 the height of an average character in the current font. Dialog units are useful because they enable dialog windows to scale up or down proportionally with the main font size in the window.

Controls use top-left corner coordinates to define their positions. Some use bottom-right corner coordinates to imply their sizes while others use the size of the *bounding rectangle*. The advantage of using the size of a control rather than bottom-right corner coordinates is that you would only have to modify the top-left corner coordinates to move the control on the screen. Top-left *x, y* coordinates are the starting position of a control. Bottom-right coordinates are formed by adding the starting point and the size of the object. This gives a coordinate that is one unit beyond the object in both the *x* and the *y* directions.

5.3 Colors

Every color is created from an *RGB value* (red/green/blue) consisting of three **int** numbers in the range 0 to 255. The first number specifies the *red intensity*, the second specifies the *green intensity* and the third specifies the *blue intensity*. An intensity value of 0 indicates the absence of a color, and an intensity value of 255 indicates *saturation*. Visual C++ enables the programmer to choose from $256 \times 256 \times 256$ (approximately 16 million) colors. The red, green and blue components of a color can be contained in three separate **UINT** (**unsigned int**) variables or packed in a **COLORREF** (color reference value, an **unsigned long**). The macro **RGB** packs the red, green and blue values into a **COLORREF**. The actual color that is displayed is constrained by device or palette limitations. The closest available color will appear on the display device. Figure 5.1 lists some common colors and their RGB values.

Color	RGB value
black	0, 0, 0
gray	128, 128, 128
light gray	192, 192, 192

Fig. 5.1   Some common RGB values (part 1 of 2).

Color	RGB value
blue	0, 0, 255
cyan	0, 255, 255
green	0, 255, 0
yellow	255, 255, 0
white	255, 255, 255
red	255, 0, 0
magenta	255, 0, 255
violet	255, 128, 255
purple	128, 0, 128
orange	255, 128, 0

Fig. 5.1   Some common RGB values (part 2 of 2).

5.4 Drawing Functions

MFC provides many functions for building an image by drawing pixels, lines, arcs, rectangles, pie wedges, ellipses and polygons. Drawing functions filter all coordinates to clip an image to fit in the target bitmap, so we do not have to be concerned about checking if coordinates are out of bounds. The first step in drawing is often to clear the bitmap by calling function **PatBlt**, *the pattern block transfer*. Once a program builds an image it is often more efficient to copy it than to redraw it. For copying large areas of images efficiently, **CDC** member function **BitBlt** (*bit block transfer*) provides high-performance copying of rectangular areas of bitmaps.

Performance Tip 5.1

You can build an image in a memory device context (a device context used as a work area for building or storing images off the screen in memory), then copy all or parts of it to the screen device context for high-performance refreshing of the screen.

5.5 Drawing Properties

A device context (base-class **CDC** or a derived-class **CPaintDC** or **CClientDC**) encapsulates the objects used for drawing and provides functions for drawing. A program builds its context by creating bitmaps, pens and brushes and selecting one of each to use in subsequent drawing operations. With that context established, the calls to drawing functions need few arguments.

Drawing uses two objects to specify drawing properties, a pen to specify line color, thickness and pattern, and a brush to specify the color and pattern to fill the enclosed area. You can create pens and brushes of various colors and patterns and then select them as needed into your device context.

Software Engineering Observation 5.1

Objects pointed to by the device context contain properties that control how an image is drawn so that drawing functions need a minimum of arguments.

5.6 Shapes and Lines

A program can draw complex diagrams composed of many simple shapes and lines. MFC class **CDC** contains many drawing functions. Figure 5.2 demonstrates calling class **CDC** functions to draw typical shapes in the client area of a frame window. Class **CPen** contains the color, thickness and pattern for drawing a line. Class **CBrush** contains the color and bitmap pattern for filling enclosed areas. To draw a shape, a program creates and selects a pen and a brush and then calls a shape function (e.g., **Ellipse** or **Rectangle**) specifying the coordinates of the shape.

```
1   // Fig. 5.2: shapes.h
2   // Draw shapes
3
4   class CShapesWin : public CFrameWnd {
5   public:
6       CShapesWin();
7
8       // refresh window when requested to by the system
9       afx_msg void OnPaint();
10
11  private:
12      DECLARE_MESSAGE_MAP()
13  };
```

Fig. 5.2   Drawing shapes and colors (part 1 of 4).

```
14  // Fig. 5.2: shapes.cpp
15  // Draw shapes and colors example
16  #include <afxwin.h>
17  #include "shapes.h"
18
19  CShapesWin::CShapesWin()
20  {
21      Create( NULL, "Draw Shapes" );
22
23  }  // end CShapesWin()
24
25  // refresh window when requested to by the system
26  afx_msg void CShapesWin::OnPaint()
27  {
28      CPaintDC dc( this );    // get device context for paint
29
30      // get current window size
31      CRect rect;
32      GetClientRect( &rect ); // get current client area size
33
34      int x = rect.right / 4;   // quarter x
35      int y = rect.bottom / 4; // quarter y
36
```

Fig. 5.2   Drawing shapes and colors (part 2 of 4).

```
37      // draw a rectangle giving left, top, right, bottom edges
38      dc.Rectangle( x, y, 2 * x, 2 * y );
39
40      // create solid red brush and make it the current brush
41      CBrush redBrush;
42      redBrush.CreateSolidBrush( RGB( 255, 0, 0 ) );
43      CBrush *pBrushSv = dc.SelectObject( &redBrush );
44
45      // draw an ellipse, giving bounding rectangle
46      dc.Ellipse( 2 * x, 2 * y,   // left, top coord
47                  3 * x, 3 * y ); // right, bottom
48
49      dc.SelectObject( pBrushSv );  // revert to original brush
50  }   // end OnPaint()
51
52  BEGIN_MESSAGE_MAP( CShapesWin, CFrameWnd )
53      ON_WM_PAINT()      // OnPaint() when screen changes
54  END_MESSAGE_MAP()
55
56  class CShapesApp : public CWinApp {
57  public:
58
59      BOOL InitInstance()
60      {
61          m_pMainWnd = new CShapesWin;            // create window
62          m_pMainWnd->ShowWindow( m_nCmdShow );  // make visible
63          m_pMainWnd->UpdateWindow();            // force refresh
64
65          return TRUE;            // run until user closes program
66      }
67
68  } shapesApp;
```

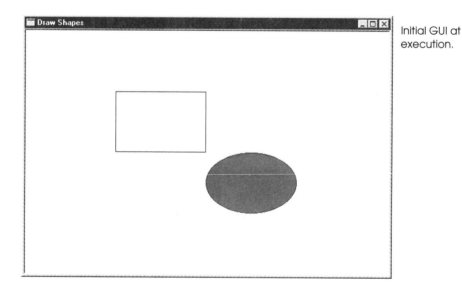

Initial GUI at execution.

Fig. 5.2   Drawing shapes and colors (part 3 of 4).

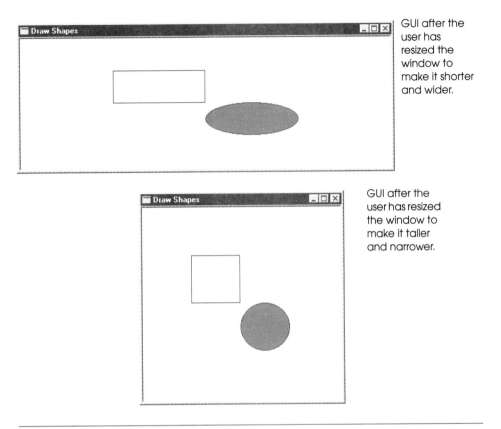

GUI after the user has resized the window to make it shorter and wider.

GUI after the user has resized the window to make it taller and narrower.

Fig. 5.2   Drawing shapes and colors (part 4 of 4).

The **CShapesWin** class definition (line 4) has two **public** member functions—a constructor and a message handler—followed by macro **DECLARE_MESSAGE_MAP()**.

The constructor (line 19) initializes the window. Line 21 calls function **Create** to create the window.

Message handler **OnPaint** (line 26) is called to "paint" the window when the **WM_PAINT** message occurs. Lines 31 through 35

```
CRect rect;
GetClientRect( &rect );  // get current client area size

int x = rect.right / 4;  // quarter x
int y = rect.bottom / 4; // quarter y
```

create a **CRect** object **rect** and call **GetClientRect** to get the current size of the client area of the frame window. The member variables **x** and **y** are set to one quarter of their respective dimensions. This allows us to draw scalable shapes with coordinates that are at the one-quarter, one-half and three-quarters points in the window. If the user changes the size of the window the shapes will be displayed keeping the same proportions within the window. If the user resizes the window to make the client area square, then the rectangle will be a square and the ellipse will be a circle.

Lines 52 through 54 define the message map for class **CShapesWin**. Message identifier **WM_PAINT** is implicitly mapped to message handler **OnPaint**.
Line 28

```
CPaintDC dc( this );    // get device context for paint
```

creates a device context for drawing in the client area of our window. The device context
stores the current window, pen, brush, font and palette and provides the graphical functions
for drawing in the client area of the window.
Line 38

```
dc.Rectangle( x, y, 2 * x, 2 * y );
```

draws a rectangle using the default black pen and white brush. The default pen and brush
are set when the device context is created. The program should save their addresses when
using another pen or brush and restore them before the function exits. The coordinates of
the top-left corner *(x, y)* and bottom-right corner *(2 * x, 2 * y)* are pixels relative to the
top-left corner of the frame window. The bottom and right coordinates are just outside the
rectangle.
Lines 41 to 43

```
CBrush redBrush;
redBrush.CreateSolidBrush( RGB( 255, 0, 0 ) );
CBrush *pBrushSv = dc.SelectObject( &redBrush );
```

create a local solid red brush and make it the currently selected brush for the device context.
This example demonstrates creating a brush when a specific color is needed in the program.
The pointer **pBrushsv** saves the address of the original brush. The macro **RGB** packs the
red, green and blue parts of a color into an **unsigned long** to make a color for a solid
brush that will fill the shape we draw. Alternatively, a hollow brush created by calling
CreateStockObject(HOLLOW_BRUSH) would prevent filling of the enclosed re-
gion.
Line 46

```
dc.Ellipse( 2 * x, 2 * y,    // left, top coord
            3 * x, 3 * y );  // right, bottom
```

draws an ellipse outlined in black (because the current, default pen is black) and filled with
red (because the current brush is red). The first pair of coordinates for the ellipse specify
the left-most x offset in the window and the top-most y offset. The second pair of coordinates are the bounding x offset one pixel to the right of the ellipse and the bounding y offset
one pixel below the ellipse. A circle is a special case of an ellipse that has x and y dimensions that are equal. Lines 56 through 68 create an instance of our Win32 application.
    In addition to the functions that draw specific shapes, a device context also provides
functions for drawing individual lines to create arbitrary shapes. Figure 5.3 demonstrates
how to set the pen position in the window and draw lines to connect points. It also shows
how to create an array of points and then call a function to draw a polygon using those
points.

```
1   // Fig. 5.3: lines.h
2   // Draw lines
3
4   class CLinesWin : public CFrameWnd {
5   public:
6       CLinesWin();        // window constructor
7
8       // refresh window when requested to by the system
9       afx_msg void OnPaint();
10
11  private:
12      CBrush m_greenBrush;      // green brush
13      CPen m_redPen;            // red pen
14
15      DECLARE_MESSAGE_MAP()
16  };
```

Fig. 5.3   Drawing lines (part 1 of 4).

```
17  // Fig 5.3: lines.cpp
18  // line drawing example
19
20  #include <afxwin.h>        // MFC application framework
21  #include "lines.h"         // application class
22
23  CLinesWin::CLinesWin()   // main window
24  {
25      Create( NULL, "Draw Lines" ); // Frame window with title
26
27      // create a pen for solid, 2 pixel wide, red lines
28      m_redPen.CreatePen( PS_SOLID, 2, RGB( 255, 0, 0 ) ); // red
29      m_greenBrush.CreateSolidBrush( RGB( 0, 255, 0 ) ); // green
30  }
31
32  // refresh window when requested to by the system
33  afx_msg void CLinesWin::OnPaint()
34  {
35      CPaintDC dc( this );    // get device context for paint
36
37      // get current window size
38      CRect rect;
39      GetClientRect( rect ); // get current client area size
40
41      int x = rect.right  / 4; // quarter x
42      int y = rect.bottom / 4; // quarter y
43
44      // draw rectangle, a line at a time
45      dc.MoveTo( x, y );          // set starting point
46      dc.LineTo( 3 * x, y );      // draw top line
47      dc.LineTo( 3 * x, 2 * y ); // draw right line
48      dc.LineTo( x, 2 * y );      // draw bottom line
49      dc.LineTo( x, y );          // draw left line
```

Fig. 5.3   Drawing lines (part 2 of 4).

```
50
51      x *= 2;        // point to the middle of the window
52      y *= 2;
53
54      // create a list of points for a shape
55
56      CPoint alpPoints[] = {  // arrow shape
57         CPoint( x + 00, y + 10 ),
58         CPoint( x + 30, y + 50 ),
59         CPoint( x + 10, y + 50 ),
60         CPoint( x + 10, y + 70 ),
61         CPoint( x - 10, y + 70 ),
62         CPoint( x - 10, y + 50 ),
63         CPoint( x - 30, y + 50 ),
64         CPoint( x + 00, y + 10 )
65      };
66      const int POLY_POINTS        // array size
67         = sizeof( alpPoints ) / sizeof( alpPoints[ 0 ] );
68
69      // select solid green brush, saving default brush
70      CBrush *pBrushSv = dc.SelectObject( &m_greenBrush );
71
72      // select red pen, saving default pen
73      CPen *pPenSv = dc.SelectObject( &m_redPen );
74
75      // display a polygon from a list of points
76      dc.Polygon( alpPoints, POLY_POINTS );
77
78      // restore default pen and brush
79      dc.SelectObject( pBrushSv );
80      dc.SelectObject( pPenSv );
81   }
82
83   BEGIN_MESSAGE_MAP( CLinesWin, CFrameWnd )
84      ON_WM_PAINT()       // OnPaint() when screen changes
85   END_MESSAGE_MAP()
86
87   class CDrawApp : public CWinApp {
88   public:
89
90      BOOL InitInstance()
91      {
92         m_pMainWnd = new CLinesWin;            // create window
93         m_pMainWnd->ShowWindow( m_nCmdShow );  // make visible
94         m_pMainWnd->UpdateWindow();            // force refresh
95         return TRUE;           // run until user closes program
96      }
97
98   } linesApp;
```

Fig. 5.3   Drawing lines (part 3 of 4).

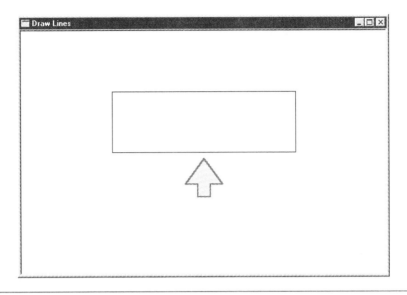

Fig. 5.3   Drawing lines (part 4 of 4).

The constructor (line 23) initializes the frame window and a pen with special line properties. Lines 28 and 29

```
m_redPen.CreatePen( PS_SOLID, 2, RGB( 255, 0, 0 ) ); // red
m_greenBrush.CreateSolidBrush( RGB( 0, 255, 0 ) ); // green
```

call **CreatePen** and **CreateSolidBrush** to make the pen and brush as data members for use by the **OnPaint** function. **CreatePen** creates the underlying Windows GDI pen for the MFC pen **m_redPen** that draws solid lines (**PS_SOLID**), 2 pixels wide, in red. Preparing pens and brushes as data members saves the time required to create and destroy them every time **OnPaint** is called. There are no MFC or Windows predefined RGB color symbols, so we use the Windows GDI macro **RGB** to make colors as we need them.

To demonstrate drawing one line at a time, lines 45 to 49

```
dc.MoveTo( x, y );          // set starting point
dc.LineTo( 3 * x, y );      // draw top line
dc.LineTo( 3 * x, 2 * y ); // draw right line
dc.LineTo( x, 2 * y );      // draw bottom line
dc.LineTo( x, y );          // draw left line
```

draw lines to form a rectangle. Function **MoveTo** sets the current drawing point in the device context **dc**. The four calls to function **LineTo** draw lines from the current drawing point to the specified point in the bitmap and update the current drawing point. The first call to function **LineTo** draws the top edge of the rectangle, the next draws the right side, the next draws the bottom and the last draws the left side.

Line 66

```
const int POLY_POINTS           // array size
    = sizeof( alpPoints ) / sizeof( alpPoints[ 0 ] );
```

defines a constant **POLY_POINTS** to be the count of elements in the **alpPoints** array.

To display a filled polygon, lines 56 through 65 create and initialize an array of **CPoint** objects. Lines 70 to 76 select the green brush and the red pen for the device context to use and call function ***Polygon*** passing the array of points and the number of entries in the array. If the first and last points are not equal, **Polygon** closes the shape. Alternatively, function ***Polyline*** does not connect the last point to the first point.

5.7 Timers

The example programs in this chapter so far have drawn an image in a window and then responded by updating the window when the user changed the size of the window. Dynamic changes to a window that do not rely on a user action can be driven by time. A program can start a *timer* that periodically sends a message to a window. This allows the program to update the window without waiting for the user to perform some action that sends a message. The window's ***OnTimer*** message handler function runs when the timer message arrives. Only one timer message at a time will be sent to a window so that if a program does not process timer messages as fast as the timer ticks, messages will not accumulate. Once started by a call to function ***SetTimer***, a timer continues to send **WM_TIMER** messages to the window until stopped by a call to function ***KillTimer***. A timer is used for animated graphics to redraw moving objects many times per second in order to give the viewer the impression of continuous motion.

Figure 5.4 draws a line of text that continuously changes color and a 256-by-256 pixel square that has a different color in each pixel. In this example, a timer ticks every 30 milliseconds and sends a message to the application to update the color of the text. Recalculating the colors square for every screen update would be too slow and would result in an unacceptable screen flicker. To avoid that problem, the program makes a memory bitmap image of the square once and copies it into the screen image on each update.

```
1   // Fig. 5.4: colors.h
2   // Draw with many colors
3
4   class CColorsWin : public CFrameWnd {
5   public:
6      CColorsWin();
7
8      // refresh window when requested to by the system
9      afx_msg void OnPaint();
10
11     // cyclic timer tells when to update colors
12     afx_msg void OnTimer();
13
14     // release resources at end of program
15     afx_msg void OnDestroy();
16
17  private:
18     // draw a colorful square a pixel at a time
19     void colorSquare();
20
```

Fig. 5.4   *Drawing with multiple colors (part 1 of 6).*

```
21      char *m_lpszText;       // text to draw
22      int m_nLength;          // text length
23
24      int m_cRed;             // red component of a color
25      int m_cGreen;           // green component of a color
26      int m_cBlue;            // blue component of a color
27
28      CDC m_memDC;            // memory device context
29      CBitmap m_bitmap;       // memory bitmap
30
31      DECLARE_MESSAGE_MAP()
32  };
```

Fig. 5.4   Drawing with multiple colors (part 2 of 6).

```
33  // Fig 5.4: colors.cpp
34  // Draw with many colors example
35  #include <afxwin.h>
36  #include "colors.h"
37
38  CColorsWin::CColorsWin()
39  {
40      Create( NULL, "Draw with many colors" );
41
42      m_lpszText = "DYNAMIC COLORS";
43      m_nLength = strlen( m_lpszText );
44      m_cRed = m_cGreen = m_cBlue = 0;
45
46      // get physical screen limits
47      int xMax = GetSystemMetrics( SM_CXSCREEN );
48      int yMax = GetSystemMetrics( SM_CYSCREEN );
49
50      CClientDC dc( this );    // get client area device context
51
52      // create a memory device context and bitmap to save
53      // the color square so it can be copied quickly
54      m_memDC.CreateCompatibleDC( &dc );
55      m_bitmap.CreateCompatibleBitmap( &dc, xMax, yMax );
56      m_memDC.SelectObject( &m_bitmap );
57      colorSquare();      // compute once rather than on each tick
58  }  // end CColorsWin()
59
60  // draw a colorful square a pixel at a time
61  void CColorsWin::colorSquare()
62  {
63      // step through red intensity values
64      for ( int cRed = 0, x = 0;      // red increases with x
65            cRed <= 255;
66            cRed++, x++ )
```

Fig. 5.4   Drawing with multiple colors (part 3 of 6).

```
67          // step through green intensity values
68          for ( int cGreen = 0, y = 0; // green increases with y
69                  cGreen <= 255;
70                  cGreen++, y++ )
71          {
72              // make blue balance the average of red and green
73              int cBlue = 255 - ( cRed + cGreen ) / 2;
74
75              // set pixel (x,y) to RGB value
76              m_memDC.SetPixel( x, y, RGB( cRed, cGreen, cBlue ) );
77          }
78  }
79
80  // refresh window when requested to by the system
81  afx_msg void CColorsWin::OnPaint()
82  {
83      CPaintDC dc( this );    // get device context for paint
84
85      // get current window size
86      CRect rect;
87      GetClientRect( rect );    // get current client area size
88
89      int x = rect.right / 2;   // middle x
90      int y = rect.bottom / 4;  // quarter y
91
92      // display text with dynamically changing colors
93      dc.SetTextColor( RGB( m_cRed, m_cGreen, m_cBlue ) );
94      dc.SetBkColor( RGB( 255, 255, 255 ) );
95      dc.TextOut( x - 60, y / 2, m_lpszText, m_nLength );
96
97      x -= 128;     // center 256 pixel square in window
98      y += 10;      // color square position
99
100     // copy color square from memory bitmap to screen bitmap
101     dc.BitBlt( x, y,                // destination
102                256, 256,            // width, height
103                &m_memDC, 0, 0,      // source, x, y
104                SRCCOPY );           // straight copy
105
106     // draw a shaded rectangle around the color square
107     dc.Draw3dRect( x - 2, y - 2,             // left, top
108                    260, 260,                 // width, height
109                    RGB( 150, 150, 150 ),     // gray left, top
110                    RGB(  10,  10,  10 ) );   // dark gray shadow
111 }  // end OnPaint()
112
113 // cyclic timer tells when to update colors
114 afx_msg void CColorsWin::OnTimer()
115 {
116     // cycle through colors in prime number steps
117     m_cRed = ( m_cRed + 3 ) % 256;
118     m_cGreen = ( m_cGreen + 7 ) % 256;
119     m_cBlue = ( m_cBlue + 11 ) % 256;
```

Fig. 5.4   Drawing with multiple colors (part 4 of 6).

```
120
121     InvalidateRect( NULL, FALSE ); // redraw all, no erase
122 }
123
124 // release resources at end of program
125 afx_msg void CColorsWin::OnDestroy()
126 {
127     KillTimer( 1 );      // release timer 1
128 }
129
130 BEGIN_MESSAGE_MAP( CColorsWin, CFrameWnd )
131     ON_WM_TIMER()        // OnTimer() when timer ticks
132     ON_WM_PAINT()        // OnPaint() when screen changes
133     ON_WM_DESTROY()      // OnDestroy() when program ends
134 END_MESSAGE_MAP()
135
136
137 class CColorsApp : public CWinApp {
138 public:
139
140     BOOL InitInstance()
141     {
142        m_pMainWnd = new CColorsWin;              // create window
143        m_pMainWnd->ShowWindow( m_nCmdShow );   // make visible
144        m_pMainWnd->UpdateWindow();             // force refresh
145
146        // start timer id 1, 30 milliseconds, use WM_TIMER
147        if ( !m_pMainWnd->SetTimer( 1, 30, NULL ) )
148            return FALSE;      // quit on failure
149
150        return TRUE;          // run until user closes program
151     }
152
153 } colorsApp;
```

Fig. 5.4   Drawing with multiple colors (part 5 of 6).

The **CColorsWin** class definition (line 4) consists of four **public** member functions—a constructor and three message handlers—and nine **private** members—one function and seven data members followed by macro **DECLARE_MESSAGE_MAP()**.

The window size is dynamic (the user can resize the window) but the physical screen size stays constant. Lines 47 and 48

```
        int xMax = GetSystemMetrics( SM_CXSCREEN );
        int yMax = GetSystemMetrics( SM_CYSCREEN );
```

get the screen size just once in the constructor.

The constructor (line 38) initializes the window. Line 40 calls function **Create** to create the window. Line 42 initializes **m_lpszText**—the variable containing the text we will draw on the window— to **"DYNAMIC COLORS"**.

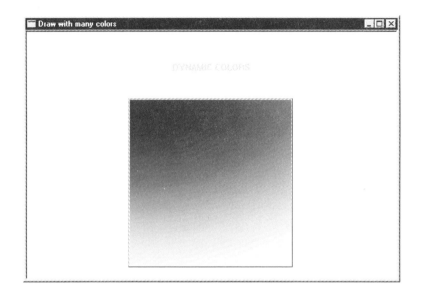

Fig. 5.4   Drawing with multiple colors (part 6 of 6).

To demonstrate control of the color of each pixel, function **colorSquare** on line 61 draws a square in which the red, green and blue intensities depend upon the *x* and *y* coordinates. The color values range from 0 to 255. The red intensity increases with *x*, from left to right. The green intensity increases with *y*, from top to bottom. The blue intensity increases from the bottom-right corner to the top-left corner as the complement of the average of *x* and *y*. The corners, clockwise from the top-left, are blue, red, yellow and green. Line 76

```
m_memDC.SetPixel( x, y, RGB( cRed, cGreen, cBlue ) );
```

sets the pixel at *x*, *y* to the computed **RGB** value. The pixels will appear with the requested **RGB** values or with the closest available color, limited by the device or palette capacity.

Message handler **OnPaint** (line 81) updates the screen whenever Windows sends a paint message to the window in response to our timer, when the user resizes the window or when the user uncovers the window. Line 83

```
CPaintDC dc( this );    // get device context for paint
```

creates the device context in a **CPaintDC** object called **dc**. Next, lines 86 through 90

```
CRect rect;
GetClientRect( rect );    // get client area size

int x = rect.right / 2;   // middle x
int y = rect.bottom / 4;  // quarter y
```

get the current window size and calculate the center of the window and the offsets from the center so we can center our drawing in the window.

Lines 93 through 95

```
dc.SetTextColor( RGB( m_cRed, m_cGreen, m_cBlue ) );
dc.SetBkColor( RGB( 255, 255, 255 ) );
dc.TextOut( x - 60, y / 2, m_lpszText, m_nLength );
```

change the color of the text string every time the function **OnTimer** updates the red, green and blue color values and invalidates the window so that **OnPaint** will be called. The background color is white. To display text on the screen, line 95 calls **TextOut** specifying the location *(x - 60, y / 2)*, the string address (**m_lpszText**) and its length (**m_nLength**).

Lines 97 and 98 set the *(x, y)* coordinates for the colors square to be centered, 10 units below the text line. We **BitBlt** the memory image to the device context on lines 101

```
dc.BitBlt( x, y,              // destination
           256, 256,          // width, height
           &m_memDC, 0, 0,    // source, x, y
           SRCCOPY );         // straight copy
```

The bitmap in the device context receives data at coordinates *(x, y)* to *(256, 256)* from the bitmap in **m_memDC** starting at *(0, 0)*. The copying option is **SRCCOPY**, a pixel-to-pixel copy from the source bitmap to the **dc** device context bitmap. The image is now drawn on the window's device context.

Line 107

```
dc.Draw3dRect( x - 2, y - 2,            // left, top
               260, 260,                // width, height
               RGB( 150, 150, 150 ),    // gray left, top
               RGB(  10,  10,  10 ) );  // dark gray shadow
```

calls **Draw3dRect**, passing the top-left corner coordinates and the size of the rectangle (in logical units) along with two **RGB** colors. This draws a square border that is 4 units larger than the color square. A *3-D rectangle* has one color for the left and top edges and another color for the bottom and right edges, to indicate shading. Consider the light source to be above the top-left corner of the screen. **Draw3dRect** makes shaded rectangles easy to implement for a new control you might invent. For example, raised buttons of a particular color have a lighter shade for the top and left edges and a darker shade for the bottom and right edges. When the button is pushed, the edge colors swap. This behavior is implemented in class **CButton**.

Message handler **OnTimer** (line 114) runs whenever the clock ticks. Lines 117 through 121

```
m_cRed = ( m_cRed + 3 ) % 256;
m_cGreen = ( m_cGreen + 7 ) % 256;
m_cBlue = ( m_cBlue + 11 ) % 256;

InvalidateRect( NULL, FALSE );
```

update the color components used to draw the text **DYNAMIC COLORS**. In this example we cycle through the 16 million colors. Each primary color intensity ranges from 0 through 255. Instead of using three nested loops to cycle through every consecutive RGB shade, we advance the red component by 3, the green component by 7 and the blue component by 11 each time we update the window. Counting by an odd number modulus 256 ensures that we visit all 256 values of a color before starting the cycle again. Using three different numbers ensures that we visit all 16 million combinations of red, green and blue intensities before recycling through all the colors again. Function **OnTimer** ends with a call to class **CWnd** function **InvalidateRect** so that the paint message will be sent to the window and function **OnPaint** will be called.

The data members for painting on the screen are shared by the constructor, function **colorSquare**, message handler **OnTimer** and message handler **OnPaint**. For this reason, the variables defined on lines 21 through 29 are **private** data members of our **CColorsWin** class.

Good Programming Practice 5.1

To improve maintainability, separate a program's internal application classes from its display classes that provide alternative views of data, such as textual and graphical formats.

Portability Tip 5.1

Separate classes for the internal model and the graphical view increase portability by localizing graphics dependencies.

The message map defined on lines 130 through 134 declares that the **CDrawWin** class contains the message handlers **OnPaint** and **OnTimer**. Lines 137 through 153 create an instance of our Win32 application. Line 147

```
if ( !m_pMainWnd->SetTimer( 1, 30, NULL ) )
```

starts a timer. The timer identifier in the first argument is 1. The next argument, the timer interval, is every 30 milliseconds. The last argument, the timer function address, is **NULL**, indicating that we want a **WM_TIMER** message sent to our application. The return value from **SetTimer** is 0 if the system could not allocate a timer. The normal return value is the timer ID given in the first argument, which can be used in a call to **KillTimer** to stop the timer.

Software Engineering Observation 5.2

If a program cannot process a timer message before the next clock tick, the next timer message will not be created. If you are keeping track of real time, losing ticks will make your clock run slower. Call the system time function to get an accurate time value.

Good Programming Practice 5.2

Use timers for periodic messages; call the system time function to keep track of real time.

5.8 Images

The simplest way to display an image is to include the file in your application through the resources. A *bitmap* contains an array of the **RGB** values for the pixels in an image. MFC class **CBitMap** encapsulates the Windows bitmap. Figure 5.5 defines a ***BITMAP*** resource, gives it the symbolic name **"COOL_BMP"** and imports the image from the file **cool.bmp** in the local directory. A full path must be given for files in other directories.

```
1   // Fig. 5.5: CImageWin.h
2   // display a bitmap image
3
4   class CImageWin : public CFrameWnd {
5   public:
6      CImageWin();
7
8      // refresh window when requested to by the system
9      afx_msg void OnPaint();
10  private:
11     CBitmap m_bmpCool;   // bitmap stores image
12     CDC m_memDC;         // memory device context
13
14     DECLARE_MESSAGE_MAP()
15  };
```

Fig. 5.5   Displaying an image (part 1 of 4).

```
16  // Fig. 5.5: image.cpp
17  // display a bitmap image
18  #include <afxwin.h>
19  #include "CImageWin.h"
20
21  CImageWin::CImageWin()
22  {
23     // create frame window
24     Create( NULL, "Display an Image", WS_OVERLAPPEDWINDOW );
25
26     // load bitmap image from resources by name
27     m_bmpCool.LoadBitmap( "COOL_BMP" );
28
29     // device context of client area of window
30     CClientDC dc( this );
31
32     // create memory device context to hold image
33     m_memDC.CreateCompatibleDC( &dc );
34     m_memDC.SelectObject( &m_bmpCool );
35  }
36
37  // refresh window when requested to by the system
38  afx_msg void CImageWin::OnPaint()
39  {
40     CPaintDC dc( this );     // get paint device context
41
42     // bit block transfer image from memory DC to paint DC
43     dc.BitBlt( 0, 0, 300, 300, &m_memDC, 0, 0, SRCCOPY );
44  }
45
46  BEGIN_MESSAGE_MAP( CImageWin, CFrameWnd )
47     ON_WM_PAINT()
48  END_MESSAGE_MAP()
49
```

Fig. 5.5   Displaying an image (part 2 of 4).

```
50
51   class CImageApp : public CWinApp {
52   public:
53
54      BOOL InitInstance()
55      {
56         m_pMainWnd = new CImageWin;          // create window
57         m_pMainWnd->ShowWindow( m_nCmdShow ); // make visible
58         m_pMainWnd->UpdateWindow();          // force refresh
59
60         return TRUE;
61      }
62   } imageApp;
```

Fig. 5.5   Displaying an image (part 3 of 4).

```
63   // Fig. 5.5: image.rc
64   // bitmap image resource file
65
66   // bitmap name BITMAP file name
67   COOL_BMP BITMAP cool.bmp
```

Fig. 5.5   Displaying an image (part 4 of 4).

The **CImageWin** class definition (line 4) consists of two **public** member functions—a constructor and a message handler—and three **private** members—**m_bmpCool** and **m_memDC**—followed by macro **DECLARE_MESSAGE_MAP()**.

The constructor (lines 21) initializes the window. Line 24 calls function **Create** to create the window. Line 27

```
      m_bmpCool.LoadBitmap( "COOL_BMP" );
```

calls **CBitmap** function *LoadBitmap* to load into memory the bitmap named **COOL_BMP** in the resource file (lines 63 through 67). The device context for the client area, **dc**, is created on line 30. Line 33

```
      m_memDC.CreateCompatibleDC( &dc );
```

creates a *memory device context*, a device context object that is not associated with a dis-play device, for storing an image. **CDC** function ***CreateCompatibleDC*** takes a device context as an argument and creates a memory device context that is similar. Line 34

```
m_memDC.SelectObject( &m_bmpCool );
```

calls **CDC** member function ***SelectObject*** to make **m_bmpCool** the current bitmap in the memory device context.

Message handler **OnPaint** (lines 38 through 44) is called to "paint" the window when the **WM_PAINT** message occurs. We **BitBlt** the memory image to the device context on line 43

```
dc.BitBlt( 0, 0, 300, 300, &m_memDC, 0, 0, SRCCOPY );
```

The bitmap in the device context receives data at coordinates *(0, 0)* to *(300, 300)* from the bitmap in **m_memDC** starting at *(0, 0)*. The copying option is **SRCCOPY**, a pixel-to-pixel copy from the source bitmap to the **dc** device context bitmap. The image is now drawn on the window's device context.

Performance Tip 5.2

BitBlt *is most efficient when dealing with data sizes that are multiples of 8 because wide data paths can be used and internal shifting and masking steps can be skipped.*

Lines 46 through 48 define the message map for **CImageWin**. Message identifier **WM_PAINT** is implicitly mapped to message handler **OnPaint**. Lines 51 through 62 create an instance of our Win32 application.

The resource file (lines 63 through 67) contains the line

```
COOL_BMP BITMAP cool.bmp
```

which gives the name of the ***BITMAP*** file on disk (i.e., **cool.bmp**). Programmer-defined name **COOL_BMP** is used by the program to refer to this resource (e.g., line 27).

5.9 Fonts

We have already controlled the color and position on the window for text being displayed by an MFC program. The programmer can also specify the font name (e.g., Arial or Times New Roman), size, italic and weight (e.g., light, bold or heavy). Large text can draw the reader's attention to important topics and then smaller text can present more information. Italic and bold text can emphasize important words. An MFC program can use the default font or a predefined *stock font* or can create one or more font objects that can be selected as needed by the device context. Creating a **CFont** object does not create a new font; it mere-ly selects an existing font on your system that matches your specifications.

Figure 5.6 contains an array of pointers to strings for sample data. The last pointer in the array is **NULL** to terminate the **for** loop that displays the lines of text. Text is displayed on the screen one line at a time. If there are **'\n'** characters in your text, your code must handle the line breaks by displaying text preceding the new line character, advancing the position down the screen and displaying the subsequent text.

MFC class ***CFont*** encapsulates a Windows font and provides functions for creating the font. To draw text in a certain font, first create the font and then select it. All text drawn on the window will use that font until it is superseded by selecting another font.

```
1    // Fig. 5.6: CFontWin.h
2    // manipulate fonts
3    class CFontWin : public CFrameWnd {
4    public:
5       CFontWin();
6
7       // refresh window when requested to by the system
8       afx_msg void OnPaint();
9
10   private:
11      CFont m_sysFont;        // system font
12      CFont m_italicFont;     // italic font
13
14      DECLARE_MESSAGE_MAP()
15   };
```

Fig. 5.6   Using fonts (part 1 of 4).

```
16   // Fig. 5.6: fonts.cpp
17   // manipulate fonts
18   #include <afxwin.h>
19   #include "CFontWin.h"
20
21   CFontWin::CFontWin()
22   {
23      // finish Windows frame in MFC CFrameWnd
24      Create( NULL, "Font Example" );
25
26      // create client area device context for this window
27      CClientDC dc( this );
28
29      // make default font
30      m_sysFont.CreateStockObject( SYSTEM_FONT );
31
32      // make 32 bit high bold italic font
33      m_italicFont.CreateFont( 32, 0, 0, 0, FW_BOLD, 1, 0, 0, 0,
34                               0, 0, 0, 0, "Times New Roman" );
35   }
36
37   // refresh window when requested to by the system
38   afx_msg void CFontWin::OnPaint()
39   {
40      static char *aText[] =      // sample text to display
41      {
42         "Welcome to C++ and MFC!",
43         " ",
44         "Height is 32 pixels.",
45         "Font weight is Bold.",
46         "Italic is set.",
47         "Face name is Times New Roman.",
48         NULL
49      };
```

Fig. 5.6   Using fonts (part 2 of 4).

```
50
51      CPaintDC dc( this );      // get paint device context
52
53      // select italic font for text display
54      CFont *pFontSv = dc.SelectObject( &m_italicFont );
55
56      int x = 10;    // top margin
57      int y = 10;    // left margin
58
59      // display lines of text centered in region of screen
60      for ( int nLine = 0; aText[ nLine ] != 0; nLine++ )
61      {
62          int nLength = strlen( aText[ nLine ] );
63
64          // get size of text in current font
65          CSize nCSizeText
66              = dc.GetTextExtent( aText[ nLine ], nLength );
67
68          // set text color, display text at computed position
69          dc.SetTextColor( RGB( 255, 64, 64 ) ); // light red text
70          dc.TextOut( x, y, aText[ nLine ], nLength );
71
72          y += nCSizeText.cy;  // advance to next line
73      }
74
75      char *lpszText = "This line uses SYSTEM_FONT.";
76
77      // select system font for text display
78      dc.SelectObject( &m_sysFont );
79      dc.SetTextColor( RGB( 0, 0, 0 ) );  // black text
80      y += 20;        // space down the screen
81      dc.TextOut( 10, y, lpszText, strlen( lpszText ) );
82      dc.SelectObject( pFontSv );    // original font
83  }
84
85  BEGIN_MESSAGE_MAP( CFontWin, CFrameWnd )
86      ON_WM_PAINT()
87  END_MESSAGE_MAP()
88
89
90  class CFontApp : public CWinApp {
91  public:
92
93      BOOL InitInstance()
94      {
95          m_pMainWnd = new CFontWin;              // create window
96          m_pMainWnd->ShowWindow( m_nCmdShow );  // make visible
97          m_pMainWnd->UpdateWindow();            // force refresh
98          return TRUE;
99      }
100
101 } fontApp;
```

Fig. 5.6   Using fonts (part 3 of 4).

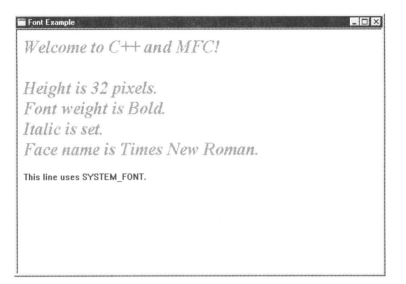

Fig. 5.6 Using fonts (part 4 of 4).

Class **CFontWin** definition (line 3) consists of two **public** member functions—a constructor and a message handler—and two **private** members—**m_sysFont** and **m_italicFont**—followed by macro **DECLARE_MESSAGE_MAP()**.

The constructor (line 21) initializes the window. Line 24 calls function **Create** to create the Windows GDI window. Line 30

```
m_sysFont.CreateStockObject( SYSTEM_FONT );
```

calls Windows class **CGdiObject** function *CreateStockObject* to create a **CFont** from a predefined *stock object*, using the symbol *SYSTEM_FONT*. The default system font is a sans-serif font.

Class *CFont* function *CreateFont* creates a font object for the program to use by searching the available fonts on the system according to the selection criteria in the argument list. Line 33

```
m_italicFont.CreateFont( 32, 0, 0, 0, FW_BOLD, 1, 0, 0, 0,
                         0, 0, 0, 0, "Times New Roman" );
```

creates **m_italicFont**. The function call requires 14 arguments but we are giving specific values for only the four most frequently used arguments and defaulting the rest. The rest are beyond the scope of this book, but are documented in the online help for class **CFont** function **CreateFont**. The first argument, **32**, is the height in logical units, which by default are pixels. The fifth argument, **FW_BOLD**, is the font weight. The sixth argument, **1**, sets italic. The last argument, **"Times New Roman"**, is the font name. This can be any font name on your system or **0**, the default, to use the system font. The font used if the font name given to **CreateFont** cannot be found, has serifs. All 14 arguments to **CreateFont** must be given, but each has a default value of **0**.

Message handler **OnPaint** (line 38) is called to "paint" the window when the **WM_PAINT** message occurs. Lines 40 through 49 declare and initialize array **aText**. The strings assigned to **aText** are the strings we draw on the window.

Line 54

```
CFont *pFontsv = dc.SelectObject( &m_italicFont );
```

sets **m_italicFont** as the font for text drawn on the device context.

The **for** loop (line 60) "walks" through **aText** drawing each of **aText**'s strings in the window's client area.

Line 75 declares and initializes **lpszText** to the string we will display in the system font. Lines 78 through 81 call function **SelectObject** to change the font from **m_italicFont** to **m_sysFont**, call function **SetTextColor** to change the drawing color from red to black, increment the vertical drawing coordinate **y** and call function **TextOut** to display **lpszText**. Line 82 reverts to the original font.

Lines 85 through 87 define the message map for **CFontWin**. Message identifier **WM_PAINT** is implicitly mapped to message handler **OnPaint**. Lines 90 through 101 create an instance of our Win32 application.

5.10 Closing Remarks

Thank you for using this book to develop a basic understanding of MFC programming. You have learned how to use the MFC classes that provide the framework upon which you build Visual C++ 6, GUI-based applications. You have designed menus and dialog windows using various MFC controls and described them in resource definition statements. You have defined message maps and message-handler functions. You have used the online documentation to learn about the controls in this book and you know how to use that documentation to explore other MFC controls. You have used device contexts and their functions to draw graphics and control text fonts, styles and colors.

We would greatly appreciate your comments, criticisms, corrections and suggestions. Please address all correspondence to our email address, **deitel@deitel.com**.

Good luck with Visual C++ 6 and your further exploration of MFC programming!

Summary

- An MFC device context provides functions for drawing and contains data members that keep track of bitmaps, pens, brushes and color palettes.

- When a function in a window class needs to draw in that window, it creates a **CClientDC** object to write in the client area of the window. Function **OnPaint** for a window creates a **CPaintDC** object to access the region of the window that needs to be updated.

- Each pixel has a color and a physical position or address on the screen. A coordinate system defines the origin *(0,0)*, the orientation and scale units, etc.

- Device units are physical pixels or dots counted from left to right and top to bottom of the screen (or other device). Logical units are counted relative to the top-left corner of a window. Logical units can be pixels (the default), English (1/100th or 1/1000th of an inch) or metric (1/10th or 1/100th of a millimeter) units.

- Dialog units enable dialogs to scale up or down proportionally with the window's font size.

- Every color is created from an RGB value (red/green/blue) consisting of three **int** numbers in the range 0 to 255. The first number specifies the red intensity, the second specifies the green intensity and the third specifies the blue intensity. Visual C++ enables the programmer to choose from approximately 16 million colors.

- The red, green and blue components of a color can be contained in three separate **UINT** variables or packed in a **COLORREF**. Macro **RGB** packs the red, green and blue values into a **COLORREF**. The actual color that is displayed is constrained by device or palette limitations.

- MFC provides functions for building an image by drawing pixels, lines, arcs, rectangles, pie wedges, ellipses and polygons. All coordinates are filtered to clip an image to fit in the target bitmap.

- For copying large areas of images efficiently, **CDC** member function **BitBlt** (bit block transfer) provides high-performance copying of rectangular areas of bitmaps.

- Drawing uses two objects to specify drawing properties, a pen to specify line color, thickness and pattern, and a brush to specify the color and pattern to fill the enclosed area.

- Class **CDC** contains drawing functions. Class **CDC** contains functions for drawing shapes in the client area of a frame window. Class **CPen** contains the color, thickness and pattern for drawing. Class **CBrush** contains the color and bitmap pattern for filling enclosed areas.

- Function **GetClientRect** returns the size of a window's client area.

- Calling **CreateStockObject(HOLLOW_BRUSH)** prevents filling an enclosed region.

- The first pair of coordinates for an ellipse specify the left x offset in the window and the top y offset. The second pair of coordinates are the bounding x offset one pixel to the right of the ellipse and the bounding y offset one pixel below the ellipse. A circle is a special case of an ellipse that has x and y dimensions that are equal.

- Functions **CreatePen** and **CreateSolidBrush** create pen and brush objects, respectively.

- Function **MoveTo** sets the current drawing point in a device context. Function **LineTo** draw lines from the one point to another point.

- Function **Polygon** draws a closed polygon. Function **Polyline** draws an open polygon.

- A timer periodically sends a message to a window. Message handler **OnTimer** executes when a timer message arrives. Only one timer message at a time is passed to a window so that messages will not accumulate.

- Function **SetTimer** starts a timer. A timer continues to send **WM_TIMER** messages to the window until stopped by a call to function **KillTimer**.

- Function **TextOut** draws text on a window.

- Copying option **SRCCOPY** performs a pixel-to-pixel copy from the source bitmap to the device context bitmap.

- Function **InvalidateRect** generates a paint message.

- A bitmap contains an array of the **RGB** values for the pixels in an image. MFC class **CBitMap** encapsulates a Windows bitmap.

- **CBitmap** function **LoadBitmap** loads a bitmap into memory.

- A memory device context is a device context object that is not associated with a display device but is a context for storing an image. **CDC** function **CreateCompatibleDC** takes a device context as an argument and creates a memory device context.

- MFC class **CFont** encapsulates a Windows font and provides functions for creating the font. All text drawn on the window will use that font until it is superseded by selecting another font.

- The programmer can also specify the font name, size and style. An MFC program can use the default font or a predefined stock font or can create one or more font objects that can be selected as needed by a device context. Creating a **CFont** object does not create a new font; it merely selects an existing font on your system that matches your specifications.

Terminology

BeginPaint function of class **CWnd**
bit block transfer
BitBlt function of class **CDC**
BITMAP resource
bitmap
bitmap images
blue intensity
bounding rectangle
brush
CBitmap class
CBrush class
CClientDC class
CDC class
CFont class
clip an image
color palette
COLORREF data type
coordinate systems
CGdiObject class
CPaintDC class
CPoint class
CreateCompatibleDC function of class **CDC**
CreateCompatibleBitmap (**CBitmap**)
CreateFont function of class **CFont**
CreatePen function of class **CPen**
CreateSolidBrush (class **CBrush**)
CreateStockObject (**CGdiObject**)
CRect class
CSize class
device context
device units
dialog units
Draw3dRect function of class **CDC**
EndPaint function of class **CWnd**
Ellipse function of class **CDC**
flicker
font
FW_BOLD style
GetClientRect function of class **CWnd**
GetPixel function of class **CDC**
GetTextExtent function of class **CDC**
graphical device interface (GDI)
GetSystemMetrics function

graphics programming
green intensity
HOLLOW_BRUSH stock object
InvalidateRect function of class **CWnd**
KillTimer function of class **CWnd**
LineTo function of class **CDC**
LoadBitmap function of class **CBitmap**
logical coordinates
logical units
memory device context
MoveTo function of class **CDC**
OnPaint message handler
OnTimer message handler
ON_WM_TIMER macro
PatBlt function of class **CDC**
PATCOPY constant
pattern block transfer
pen
physical coordinates
pixel
points
Polygon function of class **CDC**
real time
Rectangle function of class **CDC**
red intensity
RGB macro
saturation
scaling
SelectObject function of class **CDC**
SetBkColor function of class **CDC**
SetPixel function of class **CDC**
SetTextColor function of class **CDC**
SetTimer function of class **CWnd**
SYSTEM_FONT stock font
stock font
text color
text font
text size
TextOut function of class **CDC**
timer
WM_PAINT message
WM_TIMER message

Good Programming Practices

5.1   To improve maintainability, separate a program's internal application classes from its display
classes that provide alternative views of data, such as textual and graphical formats.

5.2   Use timers for periodic messages; call the system time function to keep track of real time.

Performance Tips

5.1   You can build an image in a memory device context (a device context used as a work area for building or storing images off the screen in memory) then copy all or parts of it to the screen device context for high-performance refreshing of the screen.

5.2   `BitBlt` is most efficient when dealing with data sizes that are multiples of 8 because wide data paths can be used and internal shifting and masking steps can be skipped.

Portability Tip

5.1   Separate classes for the internal model and the graphical view increase portability by localizing graphics dependencies.

Software Engineering Observations

5.1   Objects pointed to by the device context contain properties that control how an image is drawn so that drawing functions need a minimum of arguments.

5.2   If a program cannot process a timer message before the next clock tick, the next timer message will not be created. If you are keeping track of real time, losing ticks will make your clock run slower. Call the system time function to get an accurate time value.

Self-Review Exercises

5.1   Fill in the blanks in each of the following:
   e) Physical coordinates are pixels counted from _____ to _____ and _____ to _____ on the screen.
   f) Logical coordinates are units counted relative to the _____ of an object's _____.
   g) Bottom-right coordinates are the bounds _____ pixel beyond the object.
   h) BLT is short for _____.

5.2   State whether each of the following is *true* or *false*. If *false*, explain why.
   a) Drawing a rectangle uses either a pen or a brush.
   b) Function **OnPaint** updates the screen.
   c) Timer messages can flood the message queue.
   d) Application programmers must carefully clip their images to fit a window.

Answers to Self-Review Exercises

5.1   a) left, right, top, bottom. b) top-left corner, window. c) one. d) Block Transfer.

5.2   a) False. Drawing a rectangle uses both a pen and a brush.
   b) True.
   c) False. No more than one timer message appears on the message queue.
   d) False. A window clips all drawing to fit its coordinate limits.

Exercises

5.3   Write a program that draws three triangles of different sizes.

5.4   Modify your solution to Exercise 5.3 to draw three solid triangles each in a different color.

5.5   Write a program that draws eight concentric circles. Draw each circle in a different color.

5.6   Implement an analog clock with hour, minute and second hands. Use a one-second timer and redraw the clock face and three triangles for the hour, minute and second hands. Use the MFC class **CTime** to get the local time.

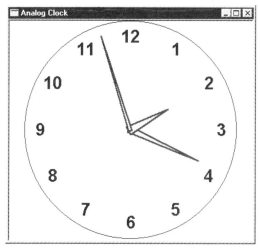

5.7   Draw a rainbow in a light-blue sky. Make a colors array from Fig. 5.1 and set pixel colors based on the pixel's distance from the center of the rainbow.

5.8   Draw a monthly calendar with lines forming the grid for the month, the day numbers in the grid, the days of the week above the grid columns and the month name in a larger font centered above the calendar.

5.9   Draw overlapping red, green and blue disks to demonstrate additive colors. Choose three equidistant points to be the centers of the disks. For each pixel in the window, if it is within the radius of a disk, set its value for that disk's color to 255. Where the disks overlap, the RGB values will produce blended colors and where all three disks overlap, the region will appear white. Optionally change all black pixels (those not within the radius of any disk) to white.

5.10   Two trains are 100 miles apart heading toward each other, each going 50 miles per hour. A bee, flying 75 miles per hour, flies from one train to the other, back and forth, trying to warn the engineers, to no avail. Simulate this scenario with one simulated second per timer tick. Choose an appropriate timer value. How far does the bee fly? Display the velocity, position and total distance traveled for each of the moving objects. Use different-colored rectangles for the trains and a small circle for the bee. Add controls for setting the speeds.

5.11   Extend the ice cream shop program to draw a picture, made of simple shapes and colors, as an ice cream cone or sundae is ordered. Use the following **RGB** values.

Flavor	RGB
Fudge	150, 75, 0
Chocolate	200, 100, 10
Vanilla	255, 255, 200
Strawberry	255, 100, 100

Fig. 5.7   RGB colors for ice cream flavors.

5.12   Draw randomly colored polygons (e.g., triangles, octagons, etc.) at random locations on the screen. Allow the user to input the number of polygons. Provide a button for clearing the window.

5.13   Implement a three-wheel, eight-shape slot machine (one-armed bandit).

5.14   Implement a Tic-Tac-Toe game board. Draw the board as four thick lines. Use a graphical editor (e.g., Microsoft Paint) to create bitmap images of a red X and a blue O. Draw the appropriate bitmap when a player moves.

5.15   Add logic to the preceding program for the computer to play Tic-Tac-Toe against the user.

5.16   Write a program that randomly chooses a shape and draws it on the screen at random coordinates. Use a timer to draw a new shape after a specified interval.

5.17   Modify Fig. 5.4 to change the message text the same color as the pixel at the mouse position. Remove the timer. Display each red, green and blue integer value as text.

Appendix A
MFC Resources

A.1 Introduction

There is a bounty of C++ and MFC information on the World Wide Web. Many people are using MFC and sharing their thoughts, discoveries, ideas and source code with each other via the Internet. The following is a list of Internet and World Wide Web resources where you will find news, products, FAQs (Frequently Asked Questions), source code, tutorials and other valuable Visual C++ and MFC related information. If you would like to recommend other sites, please send us email at

deitel@deitel.com

and we will put links to the sites you suggest on our Web site

http://www.prenhall.com/deitel

A.2 Resources

http://msdn.microsoft.com/visualc/
> The *Microsoft Visual C++ homepage* includes, news, product information, tutorials and downloads.

http://www.codeguru.com
> The *Code Guru* site is a resource for developers where you can find code snippets, FAQs, newsgroups, contests, forums and more.

http://devcentral.iftech.com/
> *DevCentral* is another resource developer site where you will find tutorials, a question and answer forum, links to related web sites and the DevJournal newsletter. You can also download ITCLib, a free extension library for MFC.

http://www.visionx.com/mfcpro/
> The *MFC Professional* web site has links to Visual C++ and MFC sites, source code, user groups and MFC related products.

`http://msdn.microsoft.com/library/devprods/vs6/vc++/`
`vccore/_core_mfc.3a_.overview.htm`

> The *Microsoft Developer Network MFC: Overview site* is an excellent resource for MFC information. You will find samples, tutorials and instructions on performing various tasks using MFC.

`http://www.geocities.com/SiliconValley/Horizon/1350/pacman/`

> Check out the classic *Pacman video game* written in Visual C++ using MFC. The source code is provided.

A.3 Tutorials

`http://devcentral.iftech.com/`

> *DevCentral* is another resource developers where you will find tutorials, a question and answer forum, links to related web sites and the DevJournal newsletter. You can also download ITCLib, a free extension library for MFC.

`http://msdn.microsoft.com/library/devprods/vs6/vc++/`
`vccore/_core_mfc.3a_.overview.htm`

> The *Microsoft Developer Network MFC: Overview site* is an excellent resource for MFC information. You will find samples, tutorials and instructions on how to perform various tasks using MFC.

`http://msdn.microsoft.com/visualc/`

> The *Microsoft Visual C++ homepage* includes, news, product information, tutorials and software downloads.

A.4 FAQs

`http://www.codeguru.com`

> The *Code Guru* site is a resource for developers where you can find code snippets, FAQs, newsgroups, contests, forums and more.

`http://www.inquiry.com/techtips/mfc_pro/`

> The *Developer Exchange "Ask the MFC Pro"* web site is an extensive FAQ for MFC programming. Submit your MFC programming questions, see responses to other frequently asked questions, or check out the extensive links for developers.

`http://www.experts-exchange.com/`

> The *Experts Exchange* site has a section for MFC programming where you can post your questions and their MFC experts will email you with a response.

A.5 Products

`http://devcentral.iftech.com/`

> *DevCentral* is another resource developers where you will find tutorials, a question and answer forum, links to related web sites and the DevJournal newsletter. You can also download ITCLib, a free extension library for MFC.

`http://www.domain-objects.com/MfcEx.html`

> *Domain Objects* sells tools for software developers, including products that support MFC.

`http://www.visionx.com/mfcpro/`

> The *MFC Professional* web site has links to VC++ and MFC sites, source code, user groups and MFC related products.

`http://msdn.microsoft.com/visualc/`

> The *Microsoft Visual C++ homepage* includes, news, product information, tutorials and downloads.

`http://www.roguewave.com/stingraycom.html`

> *Stingray Software*, owned by Rogue Wave Software, sells Visual C++/MFC class libraries. Check out some of their products or order a free MFC Hierarchy poster.

`http://www.puntoexe.com/develop.htm`

> *Puntoexe Software's CImageBuffer Project*, C++ MFC classes for image analysis and jpeg/dib encoding, is available to download free from this site.

A.6 Newsletters and Publications

`http://journal.iftech.com`

> The *DevJournal* weekly online newsletter has a section for Visual C++ and MFC news.

`http://msdn.microsoft.com/visualc/`

> The *Microsoft Visual C++ homepage* includes, news, product information, tutorials and downloads.

`http://www.rinolam.com.hk/windev/`

> *WinDev* is a free mailing list for Windows developers that allows you to share code, questions and programming experiences with other Windows developers. There is also an extensive list of links to publications and development tools.

`http://www.pinpub.com/vcd/home.htm`

> *Visual C++ Developer* is an on-line newsletter. A subscription is required to access the newsletter and the downloads, however you can access the free tips and the list of hotlinks without subscribing.

A.7 Newsgroups

`news:comp.os.ms-windows.apps`

`news:comp.os.ms-windows.misc`

`news:comp.os.ms-windows.programmer.controls`

`news:comp.os.ms-windows.programmer.graphics`

`news:comp.os.ms-windows.programmer.memory`

`news:comp.os.ms-windows.programmer.misc`

`news:comp.os.ms-windows.programmer.multimedia`

`news:comp.os.ms-windows.programmer.networks`

`news:comp.os.ms-windows.programmer.tools.mfc`

`news:microsoft.public.vc.mfc`

`news:microsoft.public.vc.mfc.docview`

`news:microsoft.public.vc.mfc.macintosh`

`news:microsoft.public.vc.mfcole`

`news:microsoft.public.vc.language`

`news:microsoft.public.vc.activextemplatelib`

Bibliography

(Bl96)   Blaszczak, Mike, et. al. *Revolutionary Guide to MFC 4.0 Programming with Visual C++*. Chicago Illinois: Wrox Press, 1996.

(Bi96)   Brian, Marshall. *Win32 System Services: The Heart of Windows 95 and Windows NT Second Edition*. 1996.

(Bo98)   Broquard, Vic. *Intermediate MFC for Windows 95 and NT*. Upper Saddle River, New Jersey: Prentice Hall, 1998.

(Br96)   Brain, Marshall and Lance Lovette. *Developing Professional Applications in Windows 95 and NT Using MFC Second Edition*. Upper Saddle River, New Jersey: Prentice Hall, 1996.

(De97)   Deitel & Deitel, *C++ How to Program Second Edition*, Upper Saddle River, New Jersey: Prentice Hall, 1997.

(Dr98)   Draxler, Laura. *Windows Programming, Under the Hood of MFC: With A Quick Tour of Visual C++ Tools*. Upper Saddle River, New Jersey: Prentice Hall, 1998.

(Ka98)   Kain, Eugène. *The MFC Answer Book: Solutions for Effective Visual C++ Applications*. Reading, MA: Addison-Wesley, 1998.

(Kr98)   Kruglinski, David J. *Programming Microsoft Visual C++ Fifth Edition*. Redmond, WA: Microsoft Press, 1998.

(Mi98)   Microsoft Corporation. *Visual C++ MFC Library Reference, Parts 1 & 2*. Redmond, WA: Microsoft Press, 1998.

(Mu98)   Mueller, John Paul. *Visual C++ 6 from the Ground Up*. Berkeley, CA: Osborne/McGraw-Hill, 1998.

(Pa98)   Pappas, Chris H. *Visual C++ 6: The Complete Reference*. Berkeley, CA: Osborne/McGraw-Hill, 1998.

(Pr96)   Prosise, Jeff. *Programming Windows 95 With MFC*. Redmond, WA: Microsoft Press, 1996.

(Sc96)   Schmitt, David A. *Extending the MFC Library: Add Useful Reusable Features to the Microsoft Foundation Class Library*. Addison-Wesley, 1996.

(Se98) George Shepherd and Scot Wingo. *MFC Internals Inside the Microsoft Foundation Class Architecture*. Reading, MA: Addison-Wesley, 1998.

(Sh98) Schildt, Herbert. *MFC Programming from the Ground Up*, Berkeley, CA: Osborne McGraw-Hill, 1998.

(Sp99) Sphar, Chuck. *Learn Microsoft Visual C++ 6.0 Now*. Redmond, WA: Microsoft Press, 1999.

(Sw99) Swanke, John E. *Visual C++ MFC Programming by Example*. Lawrence, Kansas: R & D Books, 1999.

(Te96) Telles, Matt. *Beginning Visual C++ Components*. Chicago Illinois: Wrox Press, 1996.

(Tm97) Templeman, Julian. *Beginning MFC COM Programming*. Chicago Illinois: Wrox Press, 1997.

(Wi97) Williams, Al. *MFC Black Book*. The Coriolis Group, 1997.

(Za98) Zaratian, Beck. *Microsoft Visual C++ 6.0 Programmer's Guide*. Redmond, WA: Microsoft Press, 1998.

Index

The DEITEL & DEITEL Suite of Products...

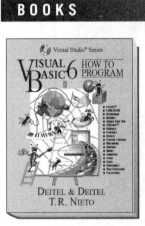
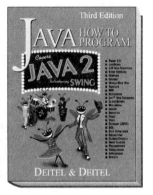

C++ How to Program
Second Edition

©1998, 1130 pp Paper,
0-13-528910-6

The world's best-selling introductory/intermediate C++ text, this book focuses on the principles of good software engineering with C++, and stresses program clarity and teaching by example. Revised and updated to cover the latest enhancements to ANSI/ISO C++ and the Standard Template Library (STL), this second edition places a strong emphasis on pedagogy. It uses the Deitels' signature "live-code" approach, presenting every C++ object-oriented programming concept in the context of a complete, working C++ program followed by a screen capture showing the program's output. Includes a rich collection of exercises and valuable insights into common programming errors, as well as software engineering observations, portability tips, and debugging hints.

C How to Program
Second Edition

©1994, 926 pp Paper,
0-13-226119-7

Among the pedagogical devices featured in this best-selling introductory C text are a thorough use of the structured programming methodology, complete programs and sample outputs to demonstrate key C concepts, objectives and an outline at the beginning of every chapter, and a substantial collection of self-review exercises and answers. *C How to Program* takes the Deitels' "live-code" approach featuring hundreds of complete working ANSI/ISO C programs with thousands of lines of code. The result is a rigorous treatment of both theory and practice, including helpful sections on good programming practices, performance tips, and software engineering observations, portability tips, and common programming errors.

Internet and World Wide Web How to Program

BOOK   CD-ROM

©2000, 1100 pp,
Paper bound w/CD-ROM,
0-13-015879-8

The World Wide Web is exploding, and with it the deployment of a new breed of multi-tiered, Web-based applications. This innovative new book in the Deitels' *How to Program Series* presents traditional introductory programming concepts using the new scripting and markup languages of the Web. Now you can teach programming fundamentals "wrapped in the metaphor of the Web." Employing the Deitels' signature "live-code" approach, the book covers markup langauges (HTML, Dynamic HTML), client-side scripting (Javascript), and server-side scripting (VBscript, Active Server Pages). Advanced topics include XML and developing e-commerce applications. Updates are regularly posted to **www.deitel.com** and the book includes a CD-ROM with software tools, source code, and live links.

Getting Started with Microsoft Visual C++™ 6 with an Introduction to MFC

©2000, 200 pages, 0-13-016147-0

This exciting new book, developed in cooperation with Microsoft, is intended to be a companion to the ANSI/ISO standard C++ best-selling book, *C++ How to Program, Second Edition.* Learn how to use Microsoft's Visual Studio 6 integrated development environment (IDE) and Visual C++ 6 to create Windows programs using the Microsoft Foundation Classes (MFC). The book includes 17 "live-code" Visual C++/MFC programs with screen captures; dozens of tips; recommended practices and cautions; and exercises accompanying every chapter. Includes coverage of Win32 and console applications; online documentation and Web resources; GUI controls; dialog boxes; graphics; message handling; the resource definition language; and the debugger.

These complete packages include books and interactive multimedia CD-ROMs, and are perfect for anyone interested in learning Java, C++, Visual Basic, and Internet/World Wide Web programming. They are exceptional and affordable resources for college students and professionals learning programming for the first time, or reinforcing their knowledge.

The Complete Internet and World Wide Web Programming Training Course

BOXED SET

©2000, Boxed book and software, 0-13-085611-8

Includes the book *Internet and World Wide Web How To Program*, and a fully interactive browser-based *Multimedia Cyber Classroom* CD-ROM that features:

- Hundreds of programs that can be run inside the student's browser
- Over 8 hours of audio explaining key Internet programming concepts
- Hundreds of exercises—many solved
- Monitor your progress with an integrated course completion and assessment summary feature
- Full text searching, hyperlinking and more
- Hundreds of tips, terms and hints.
- Master Client and Server Side Programming, including JavaScript, VBScript, ActiveX, ASP, SQL, XML, database, and more!

Runs on Windows 95, 98, and NT 4.0 or higher

The Complete C++ Training Course
Second Edition

BOXED SET

©1998, Boxed book and software, 0-13-916305-0

The *Complete C++ Training Course* features the complete, best-selling introductory book *C++ How to Program, Second Edition* and a fully-interactive *Multimedia Cyber Classroom* CD-ROM that features:

- Hundreds of working programs that students can run with a mouse click
- Over 8 hours of audio walkthroughs of key C++ concepts
- More than 1000 exercises
- Solutions are provided for approximately half the exercises, including many of the projects
- Thousands of hyperlinked index entries with full-text searching
- Helpful hints, marked with icons, that help teach good practices

Runs on Solaris 2.5 or higher and Windows 95, 98, and NT 4.0 or higher

www.phptr.com/phptrinteractive

The Complete Java Training Course
Third Edition
BOXED SET

2000, Boxed Set, 0-13-085247-3

This set includes the book *Java How to Program, Third Edition*, a complete Java Integrated development environment, and a fully interactive *Multimedia Cyber Classroom* CD-ROM that features:

- 200+ complete Java 2 programs with approximately 12,000 lines of fully-tested "live code"
- 1100+ questions and exercises over half of them with answers
- 400+ helpful hints and tips, marked with icons
- Over 8 hours of audio describing key Java concepts and programming techniques
- A browser-based display engine

Runs on Windows 95, 98, and NT 4.0 or higher

The Complete Visual Basic 6 Training Course
BOXED SET

1999, Boxed Set, 0-13-082929-3

You get the worlds's #1 VB6 interactive *Multimedia Cyber Classroom* CD-ROM plus a worldwide best-selling VB6 book and Microsoft's *VB6 Working Model Software*—ideal for experienced VB5, C/C++ and Java programmers...as well as new programmers interested in VB6's latest features.

- 6+ hours of audio explaining key VB6 concepts
- Hundreds of VB6 programs with thousands of lines of fully-tested code
- Hundreds of interactive programming exercises
- Master ActiveX, objects, TCP/IP networking, VBScript, multimedia, GUIs, data structures, control creation, and more!

Runs on Windows 95, 98, and NT 4.0 or higher

Keep reading for more on Deitel & Associates! ➤

Prentice Hall offers Multimedia Cyber Classroom CD-ROMs to accompany *Java How to Program, Third Edition*, *C++ How to Program, Second Edition*, *Internet and World Wide Web How To Program*, and *Visual Basic 6 How to Program*. If you have already purchased one of these books and would like to purchase a stand-alone copy of the corresponding *Multimedia Cyber Classroom* please call:

1-800-811-0912

For **Java Multimedia Cyber Classroom, 3/E**, ask for product number 0-13-014494-0

For **C++ Multimedia Cyber Classroom, 2/E**, ask for product number 0-13-095474-8

For **Internet and World Wide Web Cyber Classroom**, ask for product number 0-13-016842-4

For **Visual Basic 6 Multimedia Cyber Classroom** ask for product number 0-13-083116-6

International Customers: Please contact your local Prentice Hall office to order.